W9-AFU-681

D.T 1595

Pg 20
Pg 73

# Men Behind Bars

Sexual Exploitation in Prison

# Men Behind Bars

## Sexual Exploitation in Prison

Wayne S. Wooden
and
Jay Parker

Plenum Press • New York and London

Library of Congress Cataloging in Publication Data

Wooden, Wayne S.
  Men behind bars.

  Bibliography: p.
  Includes index.
  1. Prisoners—Sexual behavior. I. Parker, Jay,
1945–      . II. Title.
HV8836.W66 1982          306.7'0880692          82-12242
ISBN 0-306-41074-5

© 1982 Wayne S. Wooden and Jay Parker

Plenum Press, New York is a
Division of Plenum Publishing Corporation
233 Spring Street, New York, N.Y. 10013

Printed in the United States of America

"The vilest deeds like poison weeds
Bloom well in prison-air:
It is only what is good in Man,
That wastes and withers there:
Pale Anguish keeps the heavy gate,
And the warder is Despair."

OSCAR WILDE
*"The Ballad of Reading Gaol"*
(1898), Line 5, Stanza 5

# Acknowledgments

The authors would like to take this opportunity to thank the many individuals who contributed to this book.

During the initial stages of the project Stephen Brody and Louis Schwartz provided encouragement, counsel, and support without which the study could not have been conducted. We are grateful also to a very special person and friend, Douglas Bivens, who has been a continuing source of inspiration.

Although they remain anonymous in the text, we are indebted to the many inmates who have shared their personal experiences with us and who have contributed to our understanding of this subject.

We also wish to acknowledge the technical advice and assistance of State of California Department of Corrections personnel.

We are equally indebted to Nicholas Groth, Stephen Murray, Jay Bolton, and John Ruden for their editorial comments and suggestions. David G. Null assisted us with the statistical analysis.

Special thanks are due to Arthur Martinez for drawing Figure 1, and to Gary Howell for drawing Figures 2 and 3.

Finally, we wish to express our appreciation to our editor, Linda Greenspan Regan, of Plenum Publishing Corporation, who has offered invaluable help in putting this volume together.

W. S. W.
J. P.

# Contents

# 1

## Introduction

"Barry" is a seventeen-year-old single white male. He has blond hair and blue eyes, weighs 150 pounds, and is five feet eleven inches tall. He was arrested in California at age sixteen for assault and robbery. Because he was underage he was initially segregated in a one-man cell while in county jail. Then, upon admission to a state prison reception and classification facility, he was housed in a special dormitory for young, inexperienced inmates who would be at risk within the general population.

Upon completion of his screening Barry's counselor recommended that he be sent to a penal institution reserved for the younger, more violence-prone, and hard-core inmates. Barry said that he felt he would have "problems" at the recommended facility, but his counselor replied, "You won't have any problems." Once he arrived, Barry was double-celled with a nineteen-year-old inmate who beat and anally raped him during his first night in the admission unit. Barry's cellmate continued to assault him sexually during the two weeks they were housed together. After being transferred from the admission unit into the general population Barry shared a cell with a thirty-year-old inmate who felt sorry for him and agreed to protect him. Although this cellmate did not use Barry sexually, he gave the impression to the other inmates that Barry was his "kid" (that is, someone who was sexually servicing him exclusively). Approximately five months later Barry's cellmate was thrown into the "hole" or isolation area, and Barry began to be pressured for sex by many different inmates. The institution, however, was "locked down" (the inmates were confined to quarters) and their pressure was only verbal, since they did not have physical access to him. At this point Barry was taken before a classification hearing. In response to his claims of sexual assault and harassment, one of the staff members stated, "I don't feel sorry for you. You're getting what you deserve. You assaulted and robbed a man, and now you're getting what's coming to you." The classification committee, however, voted to transfer him to a medium-security prison.

Upon his arrival at the institution we investigated for our study, Barry's reputation as a "punk," an inmate who has been forced into a sexually submissive role, had followed him and he received a degree of sexual pressuring. He is currently in the reception unit, or "fish row" as it is known. Already an inmate named "Ben" has approached Barry to "hook up" or develop a steady sexual relationship with him in exchange for protection, as have several other prisoners. Barry, who has five years left to serve on his sentence, felt he had no choice and accepted Ben's offer.

During our interview with Barry we found him to be quiet, sensitive, and passive. He is a youngster from a middle-class background who does not project the image of a "tough guy." He had had absolutely no sexual experience with other males prior to coming to prison and was understandably insecure, scared, and easily intimidated.

Barry's experience is not unique. Incarceration creates a high risk of sexual victimization for males. It is a fact of prison life, disquieting to inmates, staff, and administration alike. Such exploitation, although recognized, is generally unacknowledged, incompletely understood, and inadequately addressed.

To understand the dynamics of such sexual victimization one needs to be aware of prison subculture and its code of conduct specifically as it relates to sexual behavior in prison. A variety of sexual scripts or characteristic patterns of sexual behavior is evident in men's prisons. These include the following:

- The *kid* or *punk*, heterosexual men like Barry and bisexual men who have been "turned out" or forced to assume a sexually submissive role.
- The *jocker* or *stud*, men who have sex with homosexuals or punks. Since these men assume only the "masculine" role in the sexual encounter (active in anal intercourse and passive in fellatio) they do not define themselves as homosexual, nor as engaging in a homosexual act. Some of these jockers, however, define themselves as bisexual. It is the partner who assumes, or is forced into, the submissive role and who is defined as weak and inferior. The partner violates the masculine image, and is therefore a "broad" or "sissy." The distinction is between the strong and the weak, the dominant and the dominated, and ultimately between men and women.
- The *queen* or *sissy*, homosexual (or transsexual) males who adopt stereotyped effeminate mannerisms and play predominantly the submissive sexual role.
- The *homosexual* or *gay*, men who are more diverse in their sexual activity, who assume both active and passive roles, and who display few if any effeminate mannerisms.

## SCOPE OF OUR STUDY

This study explores the sociosexual patterns among inmates that exist in a particular medium-security prison for adult male felons, and examines the various forms of male sexual activities and interrelationships, as well as the attitudes toward such behavior expressed by the inmates, the guards, and the administration of the prison. In addition we examine the impact of sexual assault on the inmates, and explore the coping strategies of the men in prison who have been sexually victimized. From such an investigation we hope to call attention to the plight of such victims and suggest ways of bringing about change so that the likelihood of their being victimized is lessened.

This concern stems from a desire to investigate the charges of brutality inflicted on young male prisoners reported in the media as well as the 1980 assertions of the National Gay Task Force that "Gay prisoners are still denied equal opportunity for recreation, education and parole; they are prevented from reading gay newspapers or seeing gay ministers; they are assaulted and raped."[1] This study, therefore, is interested in determining whether there has been any recent change in prison code and policy that might reflect the changing attitudes in society toward homosexuality and the gay lifestyle. Obviously, the institution of the prison is quite restrictive and different from other social, even total, institutions, but our research interest concerns whether or not the prison situation has remained indifferent to these external changes.

Homosexual behavior in prison has been widely discussed in the social science literature.[2] More often than not, however, these studies discuss homosexuality as a "problem" to the institution, or as a by-product of prison institutional conditions. Suggestions for "curbing" homosexual activity, for example, are expressed by introducing heterosexual conjugal visits, providing the inmates with pornography, and separating the "visible" homosexuals from the heterosexuals. In most instances homosexuality in prison continues to be viewed as a social problem and viewed from a decidedly heterosexual bias. Outside of the current research project being conducted by the Center for Research and Education in Sexuality (C.E.R.E.S.) on sexual assault in jail[3] and the study being conducted by the Federal Bureau of Prisons, no systematic study has been published which looks specifically at the topic of prison homosexuality from the perspective of the homosexual inmate and the vulnerable heterosexual youngster. There have, however, been prison studies of homosexual behavior which have viewed the phenomenon in less problematic terms.[4]

## RESEARCH METHODS

During 1979 and 1980 the authors conducted a research project aimed at studying the sexual behavior of inmates with a particular focus on the dynamics of sexual exploitation and coercion. The setting for this study was a medium-security penal institution located in California with a prison population of over 2500 men. This penal institution is one to which "known" (meaning effeminate) homosexuals are sent since the inmates are housed in single-man cells as opposed to two-man cells or dormitory-type facilities. Single-celled housing is aimed at lessening the degree of sexual assault and activity.

A variety of research techniques was employed in gathering the data for this study, including:

- A twenty-item questionnaire on sexual behavior in prison was given to a random sample of all inmates in the prison who had served more than one year. Of slightly more than 600 questionnaires distributed throughout the four quads, some 200 completed forms were analyzed, a response rate of one-third of those randomly selected for sampling and approximately 10% of the total eligible prison population.

- A twenty-six-item questionnaire on both their sexual behavior in prison and their feelings and attitudes was given to a quota-controlled sample of eighty self-defined homosexual men. This sample was obtained either through personal contact or referral, and we estimate that we sampled at least one-third of the homosexuals in this prison. Because of personal / contact with each respondent, 80 responses were received out of 100 questionnaires distributed.

- Additional in-depth interviews were conducted with thirty of these homosexuals. We sought interviews with different "types" of homosexuals whose prison experiences are viewed in relation to experiences of homosexuals found in society at large. Summaries and portions of these interviews are presented thoughout the book.

- In-depth interviews were conducted with four "pairs" of men who were involved in ongoing sexual relationships. Such "relationships" in prison involve a heterosexual or bisexual jocker who is hooked up with either an effeminate homosexual or a punk.

- In-depth interviews were conducted with fourteen "kids" who had been turned out in prison. These punks were questioned about their past sexual activities as well as their experiences and feelings concerning their prison sexual victimization.

- In-depth interviews were conducted with 10% of the "older men" (men over the age of fifty) in the prison population sample. The questions focused on their feelings of life satisfaction as well as their attitudes toward prison sexuality.
- In-depth interviews were conducted with seven of sixteen correctional officers of one building with respect to their attitudes toward homosexuals and homosexual activity in prison.
- In-depth interviews were conducted with all four of the inmate chaplains, both (Born-Again) Christian and Muslim, concerning their attitudes toward homosexuality.
- An in-depth interview was conducted with the associate superintendent of the prison in charge of inmate services concerning prison policies regarding prison sexuality.
- An in-depth interview was conducted with the deputy director in charge of policy for the State of California Department of Corrections.
- Contact was made with various regional and national agencies and organizations outside this prison with reference to their involvement in activities pertaining to prison reform.

This investigation was facilitated by the participant-observations of one of the co-researchers who was serving a four-year sentence in this institution for a nonsexual offense. The co-researcher had the full cooperation of both the prison staff and the inmates in conducting the study and worked under the supervision of the senior researcher. Trained as a social science researcher prior to his incarceration, the co-researcher was able to conduct the interviews and distribute the questionnaires from the role of a prison "insider." While conducting the interviews, he explained that he was part of a team doing research on sexuality in general, and homosexuality in prison in particular, and he assured the respondents that their identities would be kept strictly anonymous. All names and identifying characteristics have been altered in this study in accord with this guarantee of anonymity. The prison also remains unidentified.

The co-researcher personally solicited the respondents for the interviews with the "kids" and the homosexuals by approaching persons known to him throughout the institution. The surveys were conducted by a prearranged appointment on a one-to-one basis. The interviews lasted between a half hour and forty-five minutes. A predetermined questionnaire was used as a format, but the questions were open-ended. Within these two groups, no person who was asked to participate refused to be interviewed. In the interviews with the "pairs," the same procedure was followed. The researcher personally solicited one member of the pair who was personally known to him or who had been recommended by another person who had already been interviewed. Once again, no one refused to participate. Data for the sample of older men, for the religious spokesmen, and for the prison guards were also obtained in a similar fashion. The senior researcher conducted the interviews with the associate superintendent of the prison and the deputy director for policy of the State Department of Corrections.

For the random sample of the entire prison population, the co-researcher had one inmate assistant in three of the quads who either personally handed the questionnaire to the respondents or placed it under their cell doors with instructions to complete the questionnaire anonymously and return it by sliding the completed form under the cell door of the assistant. The assistant then returned the completed forms to the researcher. The co-researcher used the same methods in distributing the questionnaires in the quad in which he resided. Allowing the respondents to return the completed forms by sliding them under the cell doors assured the anonymity of the respondents.

Of the 150 questionnaires distributed in each quad, the number of responses gathered was as follows: 51 questionnaires were received from A Quad, 65 from B Quad, 53 from C Quad, and 47 responses from D Quad, for a total of 216 responses. Of this total, 23 questionnaires were discarded because they were incomplete. In order to have a total of 200 questionnaires for tabulation, seven additional respondents were solicited in a prison college class. These inmates were instructed by the researcher to complete the questionnaire anonymously (if they had not previously received and completed one) and place it in a pile on the instructor's desk where the researcher collected them.

The prison under study is a medium-security institution. It houses felons serving relatively short terms (i.e., five to seven years) and/or felons who have been evaluated by the California Department of Correction's placement board as being less prone to violence. Because of its one-man-cells design, this prison also houses those effeminate homosexuals and vulnerable heterosexual youngsters who would be more protected by such an arrangement.

While we feel that our study and sample group are representative of a cross section of the population of this institution, it remains problematic whether the findings that we report reflect the realities in other penal institutions. On the one hand this institution likely has a higher incidence of homosexual behavior because of the policy of assigning homosexuals to this prison; on the other hand our study is likely *underreporting* certain types of sexual behavior (i.e., sexual coercion and assault) since this prison is not a maximum-security institution, where incidents of sexual assault are allegedly more widespread.

In summary, the study is based on a variety of research techniques and participant-observations employed in studying one medium-security prison. It focuses on inmate sexual behavior and the dynamics of prison sexual exploitation.

## ORGANIZATION OF THE BOOK

This book is divided into three parts:

Part I, "Institutional and Cultural Patterns," explores the nature of prison sexual exploitation, the sexual scene as it exists in prison, and racial and ethnic differences as they pertain to the sexual behavior of the heterosexual and bisexual jockers.

Part II, "The Jockers, Punks, and Sissies" focuses on the male sexual relationships that develop in prison which pair jockers with effeminate homosexuals or submissive heterosexual youngsters. Further, we discuss the experiences of the punks in prison and the sexual behavior and attitudes of the self-defined homosexual inmates, as well as distinguish between the different "types" of homosexuals who are incarcerated.

Part III, "Reactions to Sex in Prison," addresses the concerns of the inmates and the attitudes of the prison personnel, including correctional officers, the prison associate superintendent, and the deputy director for policy of the State of California Department of Corrections. The concluding chapter also discusses prison policy regarding sexual behavior as well as the impact of prison reform efforts aimed at reducing the levels of sexual exploitation in prison.

# I

# INSTITUTIONAL AND CULTURAL PATTERNS

# 2

# Nature of Prison Exploitation

To present an overview of the convict subculture and code of conduct as they relate to sexual behavior will require that we distinguish between the variety of sexual scripts that are found in men's prisons—sexual scripts that are employed by the jockers, by the homosexuals, and by the punks or kids.

By first gaining an understanding of the code of prison behavior and the dynamics of sexual activity in prison, one can more fully grasp the role expectation and the sexual exploitation to which vulnerable convicts—both homosexual and heterosexual—are subjected. These institutionalized sexual scripts provide the heterosexual and bisexual aggressor with rationalizations or justifications for sexual contact with other males. At the same time they serve to devalue and dehumanize the passive or vulnerable homosexual and heterosexual targets of the assault, forcing them into stereotyped "female" roles. Thus these male victims in prison are reduced to "objects" of sexual domination and gratification, and become merely pawns in the power plays of inmate manipulation and control in the prison setting.

The concept of a "script" can be useful in organizing

our thinking about sexual behavior. Basically a script is the idea we carry around in our heads concerning the Who, What, Where, When, and Why of our sexual behavior.[5] For the most part our personal scripts are derived from the official scripts of our culture, religion, and family background. Our scripts are constantly being reevaluated and rewritten as we progress through life gaining new experiences and exposure to new values.

To a degree, prison sexual patterns depart radically from the traditional sexual scripts of society in general, and exposure to them can prove shocking and disorienting to the new inmate. As in society at large, patterns develop to serve the interests of the power structure and to maintain the status quo. In prison, where moral or humanistic concerns have little relevance, status and power are based on domination and gratification, which leads to an emphasis on violence and exploitation and a deemphasis on mutual caring and reciprocal fulfillment. For many convicts who have been socialized into this system, eroticism has come to be associated with aggression, and the degree of satisfaction derived from the sex act is often in direct proportion to the degree of force and humiliation to which the partner is subjected. In its most extreme form this sexualized aggression is manifested in outright acts of violence such as prison rape. In less severe cases it appears in the form of sexual intimidation, sexual domination, sexual manipulation, and sexual extortion. Such one-sided, dominant, and exploitive sexual encounters cause the more vulnerable male to feel victimized and demoralized.

## THE CONVICT SEXUAL CODE

The value structure of the lower-class subcultures found in prison, regardless of their ethnic background, places extreme emphasis on maintaining and safeguarding the inmate's manhood and manliness—his *machismo*. Moral considerations hold lesser weight in this perspective. The primary result of this role maintenance is an extreme dichotomy of sexual scripts. Homosexuals and vulnerable heterosexual "kids" are categorized as female or feminine, and are encouraged or forced to adopt feminized roles and behaviors. The "marked" men who succumb to this sexual pressure are tolerated since by conforming to the role of the woman they protect (and enhance) the masculine image of the man with whom they have sex.

A further characteristic of this pattern is the distinction drawn between the dominant partner (the "insertor") and the submissive partner (the "insertee"). As long as a participant maintains a dominant role by either performing anal penetration on another inmate or by being orally copulated by another inmate, there is no social sanction against the dominant partner who engages in the sexual act. In these sexual roles his basic masculine image remains intact even though he has participated in a sexual act with another male. To the dominant partner's way of thinking he is still "all" man. This type of convict—the jocker or stud or "straight who uses," as he is commonly referred to in prison jargon—is often viewed by prison officials and correctional officers as *also* being a homosexual since he is engaging in homosexual acts. From the perspective of the submissive homosexual or the heterosexual youngster with whom he engages in sex, however, the dominant partner is viewed as being a heterosexual (or straight "trade"). For both partners in the sexual act the dominant partner is viewed as maintaining a masculine identity. The jocker's sexual behavior therefore can be viewed as *situational* homosexuality. He attempts to replicate his sexual role outside of prison by exploiting the vulnerable homosexual and/or heterosexual inmate inside prison, treating his sexual partner as a surrogate female.

What develops is an *ambiguity of labels*. The jocker sees himself as either heterosexual or bisexual, his submissive partner sees him as heterosexual, and the prison guards consider him homosexual. Because of this ambiguity, when we refer to an inmate's sexual orientation we are using the inmate's *own* subjective self-definition and stance.

What develops because of the more dominant convicts' need to maintain, and often prove, their masculinity is a pattern of *sexual aggression* and a convict sexual code which defines how sex in prison can and will operate. This code tolerates both the homosexuals and the "kids," as long as they accept the scripts dictated to them by the convict subculture. Those homosexuals and punks who attempt to challenge this role specification are often even further victimized, although in this medium-security prison if an inmate "shows some heart" or "holds his own," he is often *not* "hit upon" or "turned out" (forced to have sex against his will). On the other hand some convicts view those men who challenge the convict code as a conquest. As one such dominant jocker proudly stated to us, "I'm going to pump that iron [lift weights] so I can fuck them punks! I mean to break me a bronco."

Effeminate homosexuals or sissies, who in prison already conform to the role expectation, are tolerated for "what they are," as being "something different and apart," but they are not thought of as being equal human beings. They are accepted as long as they continue to fulfill a sexual need, and thereby are often exploited. But these submissive men, both homosexual and heterosexual, are not respected as individuals or as "real" men. In prison, one of the worst put-downs is to tell another convict that he is "on dick" or that he is "nothing but a bitch." Submissive men are often treated as commodities, to be used and then discarded.

For the heterosexual convict, his image of machismo is chronically overplayed in many ways—style of walk, mannerisms, speech patterns, tattoos, and pumping iron.

Pumping iron is a daily routine for about 70% of the prison population. Each of the four quads has an extensive "iron pile" which is constantly in use from morning to lockdown in the evening. Being physically strong and staying in shape has survival benefits; however, it has become an institutionalized statement of manhood, and is expected under peer pressure. Almost all cliques and "homeboys" (members of a given clique or gang or group) take a turn on the iron pile daily, and take it very seriously. Occasionally throughout the year there are weight-lifting competitions between quads. When body-building contests were recently initiated in the prison, the prison inmates' newspaper felt the need to caution the audience not to whistle or catcall as "it takes guts to get up there and flex your muscles while you're dressed in next to nothing."

Tattooing is another statement of manhood. Some inmates are excellent tattoo artists and earn good money tattooing. Electric tattoo needles are made from the motors of eight-track tape players. Most of the tattoos are quite garish and gruesome. They include heavily muscled and bearded Vikings, spiderwebs on the elbows, "Fuck the World" slogans, names of hometowns or barrios in large letters across the shoulders and back or stomach, skulls and crossbones, and decapitated heads dripping blood. About 60% of the white and 85% of the Mexican-American inmates are moderately to heavily tattooed. Very few black inmates have (or get) tattoos.

While the dominant heterosexual convicts are overplaying their masculinity, the effeminate homosexual convicts and heterosexual "kids" are subjected to the norms, values, and roles dictated by the more powerful masculine-oriented majority. Homosexuals themselves are denied the right to establish their own identities and roles. They are considered fair game by the other convicts, and are denied the right to be selective or exercise their own needs and desires. Like it or not, those inmates vulnerable to sexual pressure must conform and fit into the roles and expectations forced upon them by the convict prison code. For these men coping amounts to making the best of a forced situation, finding the path of least resistance.

## COPING STRATEGIES

According to our data, 10% of this prison population were self-admitted homosexuals, 10% identified themselves as bisexual, and the remaining 80% identified themselves as heterosexual, although over half (55%) of this heterosexual group reported engaging in sexual activity in prison. In terms of having been pressured into having sex against their will, our study found that 41% of the homosexuals, 2% of the bisexuals, and 9% of the heterosexuals reported they had been sexually victimized. This represented 14% of our sample prison population who had been sexually assaulted. For these men, regardless of personal sexual orientation, incarceration has generated another problem—being a victim of prison sexual violence.

For the majority of these "targets," the best and safest coping strategy is to "hook up" with a jocker, an inmate dominant enough to protect them. In fact, as we note throughout this study, the *only type* of paired relationship sanctioned by the prison code is one which pairs a homosexual or punk with a jocker. Within these pairings there is some variance as to how the couple functions or "works things out," but the homosexual and vulnerable youngster are definitely subject to domination by the "old man."

Important to this sociosexual pattern is the fact that bonding between two homosexuals (gay bonding) is *not* allowed within the prison culture. A homosexual or kid is expected to hook up with a "man." This is the unwritten law, and it is enforced. Homosexuals and vulnerable youngsters pair with jockers primarily for *protection* from harassment; sex and companionship are secondary considerations. This coded obligation of the "old man" to protect the homosexual or punk is adhered to, even to the point of violent defense.

Homosexuals and punks are a fact of prison life and are tolerated as long as they keep their place and fit the feminized stereotype. Such acceptance is comparable to the way some black slaves were accepted, and even treated well, in the pre-Civil War South, so long as they kept their place. An example of the institutionalization of this "treatment" pattern occurred at one Fourth of July celebration where there was a fun-and-games day in the yard. Among the events scheduled were a "powder puff" softball game and a 100-yard dash for "queens only."

The *effeminate* homosexuals in prison, according to the results of our survey, comprise over half of the homosexual population (56%). These "queens" or "sissies," as they are referred to, are the most apparent and open about their lifestyle. The remainder of the homosexuals maintain a masculine identity and to varying degrees are undercover with respect to their sexual orientation and behavior.

The 10% who are homosexual in prison can be grouped as follows:

- Those who stay totally undercover and pass as straight (estimated to be about 1% of the *entire prison population*);
- Those who are known but are tough enough to stand up for themselves (less then 1%);

- Those who, because of age or physical characteristics, are not as desirable and are left alone to do their own time (about 2%); and
- Those who are hooked up (from 5% to 7%).

The vast majority of the effeminate homosexuals hook up, and in prison they are commonly referred to as "broads," and "bitches" as well as queens and sissies. Many of the effeminate homosexuals conform to the role and adopt feminine names (e.g., Monica, Carol, Terri, Kippy, and one black queen named Chocolate). Although the institution will not allow female attire or cosmetics, the "girls" can be quite innovative and creative in wearing tight pocketless pants, scarfs, sweaters, pierced earrings, and bracelets.

Although many of these effeminate homosexuals have behavior patterns more indicative of a transsexual identity, only 13% of the homosexuals surveyed indicated that they would rather *be* a female. Furthermore, this penal institution under study is *not* the institution which handles transsexuals as they are sent to another correctional facility in the state (see Chapter 11).

The effeminate homosexuals vary significantly by ethnic and racial background. Based on the results of our survey, over 80% of the black and Mexican-American homosexuals are outfront queens as compared to less than 50% of the white homosexuals. As we discuss in greater detail in a later chapter, black and Chicano homosexuals are twice as likely as white homosexuals to feel that they act more feminine than masculine.

These ethnic differences are primarily due to culturally scripted role expectations. In the ghetto and barrio cultures where there is a heavy emphasis placed on machismo, homosexuals are "pressured" into feminized roles. And it is largely the influence of this cultural bias that is carried over into the prison environment and shapes the role expectations for homosexuals (and heterosexuals for that matter) in prison. Incarceration and the prison environment merely accentuate the queen role that these effeminate homosexuals have been playing on the outside. This role, however, is *imposed* on the other types of homosexuals and the kids who are turned out.

The "cult of masculinity" that defines much of black and Chicano heterosexual self-imagery is also accepted and propagated by lower-class Caucasians. These "bikers" or "low-riders" also place an extreme emphasis on masculinity, which is reflected in such behavioral traits as beards, muscles, and excessive tattoos. While the majority of blacks and Mexican-Americans fell into this category of embracing a strict if not excessive code of masculinity, only about half of the white inmates in our prison sample conformed to this code. This was due largely to the greater prevalence of middle-class whites in prison (often sentenced for "white-collar" crimes). These better educated whites do not share the lower-class culturally induced values and norms.

In summary, in prison there is an institutionalized social pressure, both overt and covert, toward feminizing homosexuals and the kids. This pattern serves two purposes. First, it sets the homosexual at a psychologically safe distance from the "macho" image the heterosexual convict is so desperately trying to project. And second, it makes the homosexual relationship *appear* to be heterosexual in that it is permissible for a "man" to "get down" with a "broad" but not another "dude."

The choice of coping strategies for homosexuals in such an environment is therefore quite limited. Either the homosexual remains totally undercover, which is difficult to do unless he is very masculine and dominant in appearance and can protect himself, or he hooks up with someone who will look out for him. To be a positively self-affirmed "gay" person, as opposed to an institutionally and culturally defined "homosexual" or "sissy," is extremely difficult. Even with these pressures, however, the situation in this particular prison is not as acute as it is in the maximum-security prisons ("hard-core joints"), according to our interviews with convicts who had transferred into this prison from these harder "joints."

There were also a few homosexuals in this prison who had managed to remain uninvolved with the prison sexual scene. Those men who remained detached had done so by becoming affiliated with the Born-Again Christian clique, and they spent most of their free time in the company of the other Christians and at the prison chapel (see Chapter 9).

For the most part, however, anybody young, passive, or feminine is going to be constantly pressured and "hit on," and often either threatened or actually physically forced or raped. The best coping strategy for these likely victims appears to be to select a partner who is going to treat them well, and not beat, exploit, pimp, or abuse them. In prison, any homosexual or vulnerable "marked" heterosexual who is not hooked up is "fair game."

## EMPHASIS ON SEXUALLY AGGRESSIVE BEHAVIOR

Sexual behavior in men's prisons remains one of exploitation because the prison sexual code condones sexual aggression but rarely condones sexual affection. Such affection, when present, is even referred to in an aggressive context as *mugging*. Some heterosexual convicts will mug (kiss) their partners, some will not. How these jockers treat their prison sexual partners is comparable to ways they interacted with their wives and other women on the outside. Some men treated their female sexual partners with affection and warmth; others were less considerate and were more dominant and insensitive.

The overriding factor within the prison setting, however, is the deemphasis on affection and emotional involvement as opposed to the physical, sexual, and status considerations. Whereas sexual and physical relationships are condoned within the convict code, emotional or affectional attachments are seen as a sign of weakness. Stated one respondent, "It's alright for the sissy to be emotionally attached to her old man since it builds up the old man's ego, but it's considered weak if the old man becomes emotionally attached or shows affection to the sissy."

On occasion emotional attachments do evolve. Any show of affection, however, is usually covert, and in most prison relationships the couple projects a very detached role to public view. A few couples, on the other hand, were more publicly expressive and would hold hands in the chapel area, the library, and on the yard track in the early-evening hours.

In maximum-security prisons the relationships are usually much more rigid. Once hooked up, the homosexuals and punks are virtually the slaves of their partners. In the prison we studied the relationships are somewhat more congenial. Here too, though, as we have stated, two homosexuals never hook up. The relationships always involve a homosexual or kid with a convict who considers himself to be straight or bisexual.

These sociosexual patterns are *not* reflected in the studies conducted on females in a prison environment.[6] Those studies point out that women prisoners tend to form family structures with articulated roles which help to stabilize the prison environment and establish a hierarchy. The emphasis in women's prisons is on building a community of supportive relationships that prove to be stable, enduring, and visible. Obviously, these social patterns are quite different from what happens to male homosexuals and to males in general in the men's prison.

Men over the age of fifty in prison, both homosexual and heterosexual, because they are not as desirable as younger men as sexual partners, are more or less left alone. If they are interested in sex at all they will often pay younger convicts for sex. A carton or two of cigarettes in exchange for sex is quite common. Usually if the younger homosexual is hooked up, his partner does not object to outside sexual affairs if they are paid for. Often the jocker will pimp for the homosexual and ensure payment. Sometimes the homosexual is forced to hustle against his will. Once again, this propensity for pimping and hustling is a carry-over from the ghetto cultural norms. According to the prison officials, many of the jockers probably had a "stable" of women on the outside. The older homosexual will likely pay the younger heterosexual (or homosexual) for sex in what is referred to as a "trade" situation. Prison sex, however, remains by and large a young man's game.

The issue of prison sexual exploitation is a theme that will run throughout this book. Although the bulk of the study is devoted to explaining the dynamics of the sexual situation as they are found to exist in a particular medium-security prison, the issues of prison sexual victimization and exploitation remain our central concern. The concluding chapter will discuss prison policy and reform in greater detail. As we turn to a discussion of the sexual scene itself, we should not lose sight of the fact that sex in a men's prison is used by the aggressive convicts as a means of control, intimidation, and manipulation.

# 3

# Prison Setting and Sexual Scene

The entire prison complex is situated on over 200 acres, three-quarters of which are used to house such institution facilities as a sewage plant, a filtration plant, two reservoirs, and steel tanks providing for potable water storage. Only 34 acres are actually used inside the fence for housing the felons.

Space inside the fence has been laid out in four areas, called quadrangles. As one faces the front entrance side of the double security-fence-enclosed facility, in front to the left is Quadrangle A and to the right is Quadrangle B, commonly referred to as A Quad and B Quad. Those at the rear of the institution are Quadrangle D (left) and Quadrangle C (right), commonly known as D Quad and C Quad. The eight housing units themselves are numbered, two to a quad, rotating counterclockwise with Buildings 1 and 2 located in A Quad, 3 and 4 in B Quad, and so on. All cell numbers in the housing units have four digits. The first digit is the building number, the second digit is the floor number, and the third and fourth digits identify the room number. Each quadrangle has two housing-unit buildings. Each building is three stories high and each floor contains 100 cells, divided into two clusters of 50 cells each in an alternating over-under bunk configuration, for a total of 300 cells in each building or 600 for each quadrangle.

There are fifty-six square feet in each cell area, thirty-nine square feet of floor space (not including the bed area) and approximately seventeen square feet of bed space. The maximum width of a cell is five feet nine inches and the minimum width is three feet eight inches. The height is eight feet, and the length is eleven feet. Each cell has a single-person occupancy. With 2400 such cells, this prison facility has a capacity of 2400 inmates, 600 in each of the four quadrangles.

The four quadrangles are separated into distinct units by the insertion of special-purpose and community-use buildings. These include the separate dining rooms for each quad, space for academic schoolrooms, community library, gym, chapel, the main food-preparation kitchen, maintenance shops, laundry, and an industries complex. The four quads surround a central area known simply as "The Plaza." An elevated walkway extends around the perimeter of the Plaza and is called "The Loop." One primary use of this "Loop" is for the carting of food from the main food-preparation kitchen to the individual quad dining room areas. At the very center of the institution, in the center of the Plaza, is a small tower with direct visual, television, audio, and electronic-locking control of all interior entryways into each quadrangle. The Plaza looks very much as one would expect a plaza to look, with beautiful flora, well-manicured lawns, presenting a very neat, attractive appearance.

After construction was completed, the facility was opened beginning with A Quad in the early 1960s. The other three quads were opened over the next ten months.

Perimeter security of the institution complex is provided by a double chain-link fence. Eight guard towers are equally and strategically placed around the inside of the

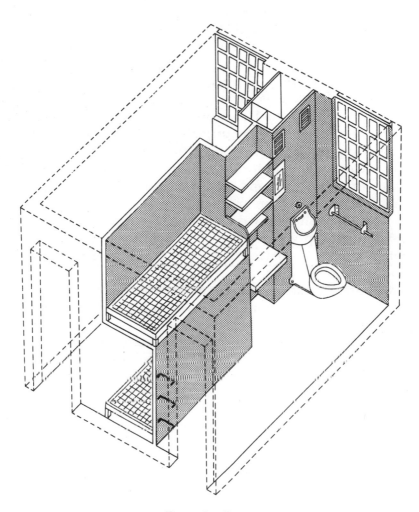

FIGURE 1: Room.

security perimeter in addition to the one tower controlling movement through the central Plaza. A perimeter roadway surrounds the institution. The two chain-link fences are approximately fifteen feet high and both are topped by a roll of razor ribbon. The security fences, guard towers, and interior building construction provide maximum security although this prison is regarded as a medium-security facility by the State Department of Corrections.

According to the Department of Corrections' Mission and Goals Statements, the primary purpose of this institution is to provide psychiatric treatment and evaluation for male felons who require such treatment, who may benefit from group therapy, and whose behavior will not jeopardize the treatment programs. Increased personal contact between staff and individual inmates is stressed. A team of psychiatrists, psychologists, and consultant neurologists offers a comprehensive program of psychiatric treatment and evaluation. Peer counseling and student-intern programs are conducted in cooperation with nearby colleges. A sixty-five-bed hospital/clinic is staffed by full-time physicians and dentists.

Programs for inmates include academic education through the high school level and an Associate of Arts degree through local community college programs. The prison is also developing a Bachelor of Arts degree program, for both inmate and prison staff alike, through the auspices of one of the state university campuses. Currently the prison offers vocational training classes in auto repair, bakery, drafting, dry cleaning, electronics, landscaping, machine shop, sewing machine repair, sheet metal, shoe repair, welding, and office machine repair. A Xerox business machine repair program is in development.

While the variety of work experience programs looks impressive, in reality, according to our informants, the programs are not as effective as they could be. Antiquated equipment, for example, prevents many inmates from learning skills that comparable jobs on the outside require.

In addition to a Central Visiting Facility providing 5500 square feet of space within the Administration Building, a Family Visiting Program is offered by the institution. Currently there are two house-trailer-type units adjoining each quadrangle. By prior appointment, averaging once each three months, inmates begin their family visits at 3:00 P.M. on the first day, continuing until 10:00 A.M. on the third day (40 hours). Participating visitors are limited to immediate family members (the program is referred to as Family Visiting rather that Conjugal Visiting as the unmarried inmates would otherwise be restricted from participating).

Only blood relatives may qualify as "family." Those homosexuals who have lovers or "mates" on the outside cannot participate in this program (except when visiting with parents or siblings). The reason for this rule, according to prison authorities, is that if they allow these men such visitation rights, then they would have to let the unmarried heterosexuals have such visits and inmate rivalries and jealousies might develop over an "unattached" female who visits one convict on one occasion and a different convict on another occasion.

## LIFE ON THE TIER

Within each of the four quads the 600 inmates are housed in two buildings of 300 each. Each building has three floors, housing 100 men per floor. The entrances to the buildings are in the middle of each complex, opening to a central foyer with stairwells extending up to the upper floors. From the central foyer which divides the building in the middle there are corridors or hallways extending out

1. ENTRY                    6. SHOWERS
2. GUARD DESK               7. TV ROOM
3. SECURED STAIR WELL       8. 25 ROOMS
4. STAIRS                   9. UTILITY ROOM
5. DAY ROOM                 10. GRILL GATE

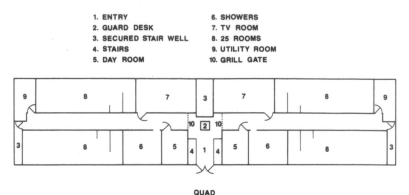

QUAD

FIGURE 2:   Building floor plan.

to the right and left. On all three floors each side has fifty rooms, a shower, a television room, and a game room. At the entrance to each side there is a "grill gate" or sliding barred gate that can be locked, separating the two fifty-man units. The inmates who live on one side are theoretically not allowed on the other side or on another floor; however, in actuality this rule is not strictly enforced.

The two buildings in each quad share a large yard and a chow hall. Each of the four yards contains a hardball diamond, softball diamond, track, tennis and handball courts, and a grassy area. The grassy infield area is kept cut and is devoid of shrubbery to prevent drugs or weapons from being hidden. (Drugs are usually smuggled into prison during visitation periods to an inmate who hides them in balloons or prophylactics in his anal cavity. In prison argot, this practice is termed "keestering" and the transported dope is termed "keester stash." Weapons are fashioned out of material found inside the prison walls.)

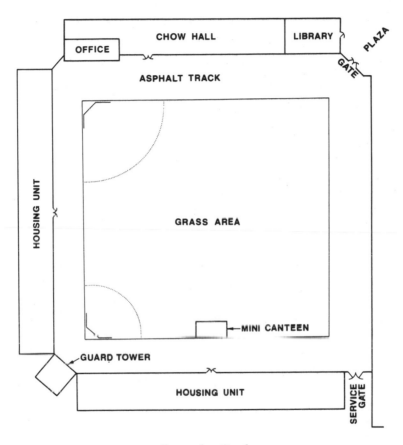

FIGURE 3:   Quad.

Within the quad there is a lot of gossip and interaction. In reality everybody knows everybody else's business, including who is homosexual and who is not, who has been having sex with whom, and so on.

The inmates are free to come and go from 7:00 A.M. to 10:00 P.M. At 10:00 P.M. they have the choice of being locked either in their rooms or in the television room. If they choose to watch television, they are locked in their rooms at 11:30 P.M.

The normal day begins at 7:00 A.M. when the doors are "racked" (unlocked) and breakfast is served immediately in the chow hall. The inmates are released one floor at a time, at fifteen-minute intervals, to prevent overcrowding in the chow line. After breakfast the inmates work at their respective jobs during the weekdays. Those inmates taking educational courses return to their cells and study or attend class. Lunch is served between 11:30 A.M. and 12:30 P.M. After lunch the same schedule is followed as in the morning until dinner lockdown at 4:00 P.M. for headcount; the chow release is at 4:30 P.M. After dinner the inmates usually "hang out" or socialize, perhaps jog a few laps around the track, work out, or watch television until lockdown either at 10:00 or 11:30 P.M.

If an inmate is classified as a full-time student and thus assigned to "cell study" status, he may, to break up the monotony during the day, go out in the yard for a while, or to the library. In the yard there is always someone "hanging around" with whom to strike up a conversation. In this prison all inmates are expected to work unless they have student status, are sick, or are physically disabled. Although some inmates do learn trade skills, this is not the primary focus of the work program.

One reason this particular institution has a somewhat relaxed atmosphere (compared to the maximum-security prisons) is that each inmate has his own room and key, and is free to travel at will within the confines of the prison. This is unlike the other "joints" where most convicts are housed in two-man cells and/or confined to their own housing areas. The inmates sent to this prison from the reception center (where they have been evaluated before placement in the penal system) tend to be first-termers or men with low-key medical problems, the less violent criminals and those men who have committed less violent crimes. The less flamboyant homosexuals are also sent to this prison whereas the more flamboyant homosexuals and the transsexuals are sent to a different institution in the state designated for homosexuals (see Chapter 11).

Inmates transferred to this prison from other institutions are those who have proven themselves to be congenial and cooperative, regardless of their crimes. Also, medical and psychiatric treatment are stressed in this prison, and the inmates sent here are viewed as benefiting from behavioral modification therapeutic programs (usually for maladaptive or antisocial, but treatable, behavior). This last group is housed in its own designated quad.

In this prison, unlike the maximum-security prisons, there is little if any violent activity or racial tension. In the two-year period of this study only nine "stickings" (stabbings) were observed, and according to the associate superintendent there have been no deaths due to inmate altercations since 1977. At most other institutions racial tensions and barriers are commonplace and there is considerable violence. Because of the relatively low-key environment, many of the findings reported based on this prison will be considerably understated compared to the hardcore facilities.

As we have stated, the prison subcultural norms and codes of conduct are rigid and traditional. Based primarily on power and dominance with the physically strong preying on the weak, the convicts settle their own disputes and handle their own social problems. The guards and prison officials encourage this rule unless it threatens to lead to overt confrontation. Patterns of intimidation, exploitation, and even sexual assault are likely *not* brought to the attention of the guards, whereas overt physical confrontation such as fist fights and stickings are more visibly apparent. As we discuss later, patterns of sexual assault can also be recognized and the prison staff could intervene in some instances.

As for the inmates, the basic rule is that an inmate never goes "to the man" (any prison official). The next rule is that one "does his own time" and does not get involved in any of the "games" that other convicts may be involved with (unless he is powerful enough to intervene and get away with it without fear of reprisal).

A racial balance, reflective of the overall racial percentages for the prison as a whole, is kept by the prison officials for each tier, building, quad, and work grouping. In this way racial tensions are minimized.

"Life on the tier" can be described as somewhat akin to life in a college dormitory, taking into consideration of course the racial and cultural divergence and the overall lower-class nature and lower intellectual mentality prevalent. But fifty men living, showering, and eating together, day in and day out, *do* develop a social cohesion and tolerance for each other. On the tier almost everyone is congenial and tends to get along. Most of the time individuals try to respect the rights of one another. At times in the television room the "vibes get somewhat mellow" according to one respondent.

Each inmate in this prison is required to have a job, except for full-time students and medical exceptions. Most jobs are full time, 8:30 A.M. to 3:00 P.M.; some jobs are part time, however, and some require round-the-clock shifts. The monthly pay ranges from $12.00 to $18.00 for institutional service-type work such as clerical, maintenance, and kitchen; and ranges up to $45.00 for workers in prison industries. Students attending college and those learning vocational trades do not receive any pay. Cash is not allowed; all earnings are deposited to the inmate's account and subject to draw at the canteen.

If two inmates are hooked up, living on the same tier is a definite advantage. Inmates living in one building are not allowed in another building, although at times they do sneak in and out. Within the buildings there is some floor-to-floor exchange; however, the building guards try to inhibit it. Movement patterns of this sort are technically against the rules, but this rule is only minimally enforced, depending on the particular guard; some guards are stricter than others.

There are four guards assigned to each building—one to each floor, plus one "rover." The guards (or correctional officers, their official titles) take a predominantly passive role in dealing with the inmates unless there is overt trouble. They are mainly "turnkeys." Occasionally they will "shake down" rooms or individuals suspected of having contraband. Usually they do not go out of their way to seek trouble. There is an open desk on each floor foyer where the guard spends most of his time, usually chatting with some of the inmates or shouting down to some of the inmates in the hallways who should, when in the hallways, be walking directly to their rooms and not milling around or congregating. This milling activity can be done in the outside quad area where there is greater supervision by the officers in the guard tower.

## OPPORTUNITIES FOR SEXUAL ACTIVITY

There is a certain amount of sexual "cruising" that goes on among the inmates. The four quads open onto a central plaza which is the central byway to the various facilities—library, chapel, classrooms, and industries. In the evening the library tends to be somewhat "cruisy" in that inmates "on the make" (looking for sexual partners) will seek each other out. Contact is usually made via eye contact and subtle nuances—much the same as on the street—and followed up with conversations and arrangements. Often the sexual act involves a quick "blowjob" behind the library stacks, or a meeting in one of the bathrooms for a "quicky." This act predominantly involves a "homosexual" and a "straight" inmate.

Many of the self-defined heterosexual inmates are very adept at cruising. This activity is steady and low-key; only the few individuals who are "tuned in to the game" are even aware that it is going on. At this prison, there are a certain number of (mostly black) straight men who have developed an "eye" or "feel" for homosexual cruising game, and participate actively in the sexual pickup.

Once two inmates have "made it" (had sex), it is easy for them to establish a pattern. After a while those who are tuned in or looking for action get to know who is available. Also, some of the older homosexuals have a somewhat regular following, and they more or less keep "regular hours" in the library when they are available. These sexual encounters between homosexuals and straights are not of an exploitive nature since intimidation or physical force is not used. Instead they are sexual encounters that are entered into voluntarily for the purposes of immediate sexual gratification and release with no or minimal interpersonal warmth or sharing involved. These encounters are basically a "trade" situation. That is, the homosexual either performs fellatio on the straight inmate or the homosexual is anally penetrated.

Often the homosexual may connect with two or three straight "tricks" (sexual partners) and they will all go off together, taking turns "getting it on" and "pointing" (watching out for the guards) for each other. This pattern appears to be comparable to "tearoom" sex (sexual activity that takes place in public places such as restrooms) or street cruising on the outside.[7] In prison, however, the sex is much more likely to be one-sided—the homosexual "services" the straight inmate who receives a sexual release while the homosexual has none. Occasionally in prison two homosexuals will get together for sex; however, this is rare. The queens, who are the majority of the homosexuals in prison, are not sexually interested in each other and prefer "trade" (meaning the studs or jockers) for sexual partners. As we discuss later, both the black and Mexican-American effeminate homosexuals preferred straight men to gays as their sexual partners.

On rare occasion, according to our interviews, a homosexual will find a reciprocating partner when he least expects it. When this does occur, there is always a warning and admonition to the homosexual not to "tell anyone about this." These reciprocating partners are not considered by the homosexuals to be homosexual, nor do they consider themselves to be homosexual. They are merely engaging in *situational* homosexual activity and are what might be classified as *pseudo*-homosexuals. That is, their homosexuality is a function of the sexual restrictiveness of the prison environment in providing for heterosexual sexual outlets. Their sexual behavior upon release from prison will revert to the heterosexual norm, or so most of them claim.

It should be emphasized that the cruising activities that have been described are not widespread throughout the prison. For those inmates interested in this type of action, there is no absence of sexual partners, either for the straight or the homosexual. Under these prison circumstances it is often the homosexual who can "call his own shots." In the words of one inmate, "It's a buyer's market."

In this sense the homosexual is voluntarily participating in this activity. Thus in this pattern of cruising, as compared to the pattern of intimidation and assault that was discussed in the last chapter, the homosexual defines the situation.

For a homosexual to get too manipulative or sexually active in this cruising pattern, however, is to bring attention to himself. If this happens he may be reprimanded by the prison staff in the form of disciplinary writeups ("115s") which, if excessive, require the inmate to be confined to quarters ("CTQ"). Or other inmates may get the impression that the homosexual is a "sex machine." If this happens the inmates will harass the homosexual, who could lose control of the situation, finding himself forced to have sex every time he ventures outside his cell.

The prison cruising scene appears to be a mutually exploitive situation. The homosexual wants the thrill of seduction and the straight partner wants a sexual release. The cruising and sexual encounters generally take place outside of the quad where the homosexual is housed. It is safer that way because someone from another quad has limited access to the homosexual and thus the sexual partner cannot be constantly demanding sex. Also, if a homosexual is hooked up, it is easier for him to sneak outside his quad and the gossip is less likely to get back to the "old man."

Living in the same building with 300 sexually deprived men creates an atmosphere of almost constant low-keyed sexual tension. And the close proximity makes it quite easy for a sexually charged inmate to approach the homosexuals living on the tier or in the building.

One informant stated that he was the only homosexual on his tier, and as such was frequently propositioned by the other straight inmates in spite of his known relationship with another inmate. Typical of what happened on numerous occasions is the following scenario: He was sitting in his room when "Larry," a young, muscled, black convict who lived on the same floor but on the other side of the building came to his door. When he opened the door, Larry asked him for a "shot" (two to three teaspoons of instant coffee; inmates are constantly drinking coffee) and started to make small talk. During the conversation, while Larry was standing in the doorway to the informant's cell, Larry kept reaching to his crotch, not too subtly, indicating an erection prominent in his pants. Larry finally asked for a "play," whereupon the informant stated that he was not into it and that he was busy. Larry was persistent, stating something to the effect of "Come on, it'll only take five minutes. There's no one around." At this point he unzipped his fly and exposed an erection, stating, "Come on, just touch it, I'm as horny as hell." The informant then acquiesced, Larry stepped in and closed the door, and the informant orally copulated him.

This is a fairly typical and not uncommon occurrence. For some inmates frequent masturbation gets routine, and when an inmate wants a sexual release the thought of a "blowjob" is intriguing, especially when the possibility is so close by. Another aspect is that almost every straight inmate feels that he is irresistible to a homosexual, and a refusal or turn-down is taken as a personal affront to his manhood. Since the informant was hooked up, had he steadfastly refused, Larry would have given up and left. If the homosexual had not been hooked up, and thus been without backup, Larry may have refused to take no for an answer and pressured himself upon the informant. The scenario described above is played out daily by different participants in different buildings throughout the institution.

The shower room contains five showerheads and is located across from the television room at the beginning of

the tier (and near the guard's station). It is semiprivate in
that the front dividing wall paralleling the hallway is solid
about five feet up and glass extends above that point. This
provides for visibility of the occupants from the shoulders
up; however, the steam from the showers usually somewhat obscures the windows.

It is rather common occurrence for straight inmates to
get aroused when alone in the shower with a homosexual,
and an erection usually leads to a proposition. Occasionally
at quiet times on the tier a hurried sexual encounter may
occur in the shower room, but because of the lack of privacy this is not common. If the homosexual is agreeable,
the participants will usually go to one of their rooms.

Since virtually all homosexuals are hooked up, these
impromptu encounters only occur while the homosexual's
"old man" is at work or not around, or if the homosexual
lives on a different tier from his "old man," or if there is
an agreement between the participants to keep the matter
private. Since gossip does tend to get around, these types
of sexual encounters must be orchestrated very discreetly,
at times when the other occupants of the tier are unaware.

At 10:00 P.M. the inmates of each tier have the option
of being either locked in their rooms for the night or staying locked in the television room until 11:00 P.M. At 11:00
P.M. the television room is unlocked, giving the inmates a
chance to go to their rooms or remain there until 11:30 P.M.
when they are required to return to their cells for lockdown. Between 11:00 and 11:30 P.M. the television room is
often vacant, or perhaps one or two inmates remain. Occasionally two inmates will arrange in advance to stay up
until this time and remain in the television room for a sexual encounter. During this period the night-shift guards
have gone home and there is only one (graveyard shift)
guard in the building. Also, the television room is quite
dimly lit. This offers an ideal opportunity to be alone, pro-

vided some other occupant of the tier does not decide to stay up and spoil the plans. Occasionally the homosexual participant may engage in sex with two or more inmates at this time.

Although the atmosphere in prison is not necessarily sexually charged all day, there is a good deal of sexual consciousness among the inmates and sex is probably the most frequently discussed topic. Pornographic magazines are frequently traded and passed around. Although, as we have discussed, some of the sexual activities take place in the showers and television rooms, most of the sexual contacts take place in the individual rooms. Even though it is against the rules for one inmate to be in another inmate's room, and makes them subject to a disciplinary writeup, frequent sexual activity occurs in the rooms.

The rooms open off a long hallway. Each room has a sliding metal door with a ten- by five-inch window in it, and a large window facing outside. During the day the daylight from the outside window illuminates the room and a strolling guard could look in the window in the door. It is not uncommon, though, to have a friend "point" (watch out for guards). At night before lockdown, with no light from the outside windows, the rooms are dark and the guards cannot see what is going on inside when the cell lights are off. Strolling the hallway in the evening, according to our informants, is not unlike the cruising activities that take place in male homosexual bathhouses. Any homosexual who leaves his room door open is inviting propositions. This can be a dangerous game because whoever stops by may not take no for an answer.

The prison staff and guards are generally aware of the amount of sexual activity that goes on. Yet the guards tend to look the other way unless it becomes the cause of potential or manifest violence. Sexual conduct between inmates is a violation of the rules, even a legally punishable felony if the guards choose to prosecute it, which is extremely rare. Generally if two or more inmates are caught in the act they receive a disciplinary writeup and are usually punished by a warning the first time, and between two and ten days confinement to quarters (except for meals) for succeeding offenses, depending on their past history.

From our observations and based on the responses of the homosexuals in our survey, the homosexuals in this prison are not discriminated against by the staff except for an isolated individual guard who may be antagonistic or homophobic. Nearly three-fifths (59%) of the homosexuals surveyed felt that the staff tends to tolerate homosexual relationships between inmates.

To a degree the staff encourages relationships because they feel that homosexuals are better off being looked out for by a partner (see Chapter 10). Encouragement means that the guards will transfer a homosexual onto a floor or to a building to be with his partner. The prison staff makes an attempt to be sensitive to the problems faced by homosexuals, but the guards' "sensitivity" is primarily motivated by their desire to prevent potential trouble. The occasional fights and stickings between two inmates (either between two homosexuals, a homosexual and a heterosexual, or two heterosexuals) usually occur over such issues as jealousies or intimidation. During the period we studied this prison, there was one incident where a newly arrived homosexual, using a razor, slashed the face of a black jocker who had been intimidating him. The homosexual is being prosecuted for assault.

# 4

# Behavior, Sexual Orientation, and Ethnicity

Issues raised in the last two chapters concerning sexual exploitation can be more fully understood by examining two theories concerning behavioral patterns in prison, and by noting what roles ethnic identity and cultural differences play in affecting these patterns.

The type of exploitation discussed in Chapter 2 best illustrates the *deprivation model* of prison behavior. This perspective argues that it is the nature of the prison institution and experience which shapes and molds inmate behavior, and that the convicts must therefore adapt "to confinement in the type of coercive organization that prisons typically represent."[8] The convict code and inmate hierarchy that develop inside the prison walls are determined by the most aggressive and dominant of the group. In this situation, aggressive behavior is often expressed within a sexual context, and the exploitation is definitely one-sided with the strong controlling the weak.

The sexual behavior discussed in Chapter 3, on the other hand, best illustrates the *importation model*. This perspective argues that the ethnic, cultural, and sexual patterns found in prison have been brought, or "imported," into prison by the inmates themselves.[9] The prison sexual scene therefore becomes a replication of sexual patterns and ethnic differences that exist among these lower-income groups in society at large. The prison experience only heightens these already existing, and possibly mutually exploitive patterns for heterosexual and homosexual inmates alike.

The results of our study demonstrate that both these processes are at work in this prison setting. That is, with regard to sexual behavior in prison there is both forced exploitation (the deprivation model) as well as mutual exploitation (the importation model). Both forms of exploitation involve the use of sex as a means of release.

Overriding these patterns in both of these manipulative situations is the convict prison code, shaped by the lower-class subculture's emphasis on masculinity and machismo which, as we have discussed, results in the pattern of extreme dichotomy of sexual scripts. Whether the sissy or punk is forced into a passive role or whether the homosexual voluntarily engages in sexual activity, both situations are regulated by the "studs" who determine the prison sexual code. Thus homosexuals and passive heterosexuals are categorized by the jockers as females which results in an adaptive process that feminizes these men. At the same time many effeminate homosexuals in prison have already been socialized into this sexual pattern prior to incarceration and thus readily conform to the role expectation that they have in part imported with them into the prison.

In prison the stigma attached to homosexual behavior for the homosexuals and kids is related to their presumed absence of manhood or machismo in playing the submissive sexual role, regardless of choice. They are *not* frowned upon because the sexual behavior is viewed as immoral.

Within these culturally defined scripts—which are magnified and intensified in the prison setting—homosexuals are fully accepted and are not discriminated against (although they may be mistreated).

By contrast, the middle-class white perspective and the Protestant religious perspective, both of which are minority perspectives in prison, are primarily concerned with morality of the behavior. The issue of masculinity is secondary. From this middle-class (and often religious) perspective, both sexual roles—active and passive—are wrong or sinful. Because the middle class places a minor emphasis on masculinity compared to the lower class, homosexuals reared on the outside from this background are less conditioned into accepting feminized roles, and these (often) white homosexuals are somewhat freer to develop their own sex-role behavior within society, be that masculine, feminine, or androgynous. Conversely the emphasis placed on the morality of the homosexual behavior leads to less accepting attitudes within the middle-class white heterosexual and Christian population, as interviews in a later chapter will demonstrate.

These social class, ethnic, and cultural differences explain why more black and Chicano homosexuals than white homosexuals behave like queens in prison. It is our view also that the preponderance of overfeminized roles among the vast majority of homosexuals in prison, regardless of race, can be explained as the acting out of culturally dictated roles and scripts learned on the outside and perpetuated in prison. Likewise, self-defined heterosexual inmates from these lower-class cultural backgrounds have fewer moral inhibitions concerning male sexual activity as long as they maintain the dominant, aggressive role. These patterns serve to explain the higher incidence of sexual activity by black and Chicano heterosexuals in prison.

## Results of the Sexual Behavior Survey

Part of our research project involved administering a twenty-item questionnaire on "Sexual Behavior in Prison." Only summaries of these findings will be presented in this chapter. A copy of the questionnaire and the tables with the data analysis are to be found in the appendix.

One hundred fifty copies of the questionnaire were distributed randomly in each of the four quads of approximately 600 men. We excluded inmates from our sample who had served less than one year in prison since we felt that they would be lacking sufficient time in prison to offer detailed accounts about their sexual experiences. By doing this, however, we likely have underreported those groups of young men who receive sexual pressure upon first entry into prison when they are most vulnerable to threats and exploitation. Examples of these pressured situations were obtained through our interviews with the kids who had been turned out (see Chapter 6). For the sexual behavior survey we wanted to study the patterns of sexual activity as they existed for convicts who had been in this prison for at least a moderate period of time. Since the entry date of each prisoner is on his identiy card (placed outside his prison cell), it was easy to ascertain the length of time each inmate had already served in prison.

As we discussed in the introductory chapter, of the 607 questionnaires distributed, 200 were returned completed and were analyzed. This accounted for a response rate of 33% and it represented the sampling of approximately 10% of the total "eligible" prison population.

### Background Information

The inmates were asked eight questions which gathered basic background information.

The *age* of our 200 respondents ranged from 21 to 59 years, with a median age of 29. This corresponded with the age range and median age of the total prison population for this prison as tabulated by the State of California Department of Corrections for 1979 and 1980. As Appendix Table 1 shows, in virtually every age category our random sample corresponded with the age range of the larger group (see page 243).

With respect to *ethnic group identification,* our random sample more accurately reflected the ethnic and racial composition of the prison for the year 1980 when there were 41% Caucasians, 34% blacks, 22% Mexican-Americans, and 3% others. As Appendix Table 2 shows (see page 244), there was a shift in placement policy by the State Prison Board between 1979 and 1980 during which time the number of Hispanics was increased and the number of Caucasians was decreased. Our random sample was comprised of 44% Caucasian, 35% black, 20% Mexican-American, and 1% other (American Indian or Asian).

Furthermore, the total number of prisoners sent to this prison increased from 2547 in 1979 to 2607 in 1980 (this figure included approximately 200 men who were housed in an adjoining minimum-security work-camp facility who are not included in our study). We have selected the arbitrary figure of 2000 as the number of men in this prison to be eligible for our study since we were sampling only those men who had been incarcerated for more than one year. (The comparative data that we use throughout this chapter are from both 1979 and 1980 prison figures as compiled by the State Department of Corrections.)

In terms of the *offense* or *nature of crime committed,* our random sample was comprised of a higher proportion of prisoners who had committed lesser offenses (e.g., burglary and auto theft) as compared to the total inmate population (see Appendix Table 3 on page 244). In other words those convicts who had committed crimes carrying longer sentences (e.g., homicide, which accounted for 22% of the total prison population in 1979) were underrepresented in our sample (only 15% of our sample reported homicide as the reason for their incarceration). In this regard, by slightly underreporting the more dangerous felon our study may have inadvertently *underreported* the prison sexual scene since it is the hardened criminal and "lifer" who are most prone to embrace the convict prison and sexual code. This is due in part to the fact that the heterosexual "short-termers" are in prison to just "do their time" and tend to ignore the inmate prison games (including the sexual ones) so as not to jeopardize their parole or release date (by getting disciplinary writeups). These men are likely to "stick to themselves" whereas the long-term inmates have nothing to lose by playing the role of the aggressive, dominant convict since their chances for an early release date are minimal.

With respect to *term in prison*, or the number of times the convict had been sentenced to prison, the figures from our sample group were comparable to the 1980 Department of Corrections figures. As Appendix Table 4 shows (see page 245), two-thirds (66%) of our respondents were first-termers, which means that they were in prison for the first time.

With regard to *length of time served*, since we excluded those inmates who had served less than one year in prison our respondents had obviously served a longer time in prison than that served by the average prisoner. Appendix Table 5 (see page 245) shows the distribution of time served in prison. The majority of the inmates (61%) reported they had served less than five years; only a small fraction (4%) reported they had served over ten years in prison.

In terms of *marital status*, no comparative data were

available from the Department of Corrections to match our sample group with that of the total prison population. As Appendix Table 6 shows (see page 245), 52% of our sample group was comprised of single men, 28% were married, 8% were separated, and 12% were divorced.

Although we did not request information on *level of education*, the Department of Corrections measured the inmates' educational level or grade placement. The inmates in this institution tested at the 7.4 grade level.

With respect to all these background characteristics our sample population appears to resemble closely the total prison population in terms of age and ethnic composition. We appear to have undersampled the convict who was incarcerated for the more serious crimes. In other demographic respects, although no comparative figures were available, we feel that our sample is representative of the total prison population, and that the data concerning the sexual behavior which will be discussed are reflective of the sexual patterns in this prison.

REPORTED SEXUAL ACTIVITY

In presenting the results of the study, we should first mention that 21 men (or 10.5% of the total sample of 200 men) considered themselves to be homosexual, an additional 22 men (11%) defined themselves as bisexual, and the remaining 157 men (or 78.5%) identified themselves as heterosexual. In the following sections the reporting frequency distributions are for the *total* sample. Later in this chapter we look more closely at those heterosexual men who had engaged in male sexual activity and the bisexual men. We discuss both of these groups and their sexual patterns by comparing blacks with Mexican-Americans and whites, since ethnic identity appears to be a crucial factor in distinguishing between types and frequency of sexual

behavior. These differences will hold true for both the sexually active heterosexuals and bisexuals. In later chapters
we discuss more fully the reported sexual behavior of the
heterosexual men who had been forced to have sex against
their will and assume the submissive role, and the
homosexuals.

The twelve questions asked regarding inmates' sexual
activity pertained only to their current prison term.

The inmates were asked a question concerning the *frequency of masturbation.* All 200 respondents indicated that
they engaged in masturbation. Twenty-eight men (14% of
the total group) reported that they masturbated at least
once daily; ninety-two men (46%) reported masturbating
three to five times a week; sixty-one (30.5%) reported one
to two times a week; eleven (5.5%) reported one to three
times a month; and eight inmates (4%) reported masturbating less than once a month.

Masturbation often takes place in the late afternoon
(4:30 P.M.) when the inmate is required to be in his room,
locked in for headcount, and at night after lockdown. On
occasion inmates will attempt to stage a "performance" so
as to be observed masturbating by a female guard taking
headcount. The administration contends that masturbation
is permissible so long as the inmate is in the privacy of his
own cell and is not masturbating in a "threatening
manner."

Frequency of masturbation did not vary significantly
by either inmate sexual orientation or ethnic identity. That
is, heterosexuals, bisexuals, and homosexuals were just as
likely to engage in masturbation. Likewise, blacks, whites,
and Chicanos were just as likely to engage in masturbation.

The inmates were asked about the *number of sexual
partners* they had had since coming to prison this term. Of
our total sample, 130 inmates (65%) reported having had

sex in prison and one-third of the prison group (35%) reported no same-sex contact.

Of this total sample (including the one-third who reported no such activity), one-third (36%) of the respondents reported male sexual encounters with only one to three occasions, indicating only minimal involvement with the prison sexual scene. The remaining group (29%) reported sexual experiences with a greater number of sexual partners. For example, twenty-seven men (13.5%) reported having had sex with four to six partners; five men reported seven to nine partners; nineteen inmates reported ten to twenty partners; and seven men reported having engaged in sex with more than twenty partners.

As we would expect, the inmates' sexual orientation accounts for a significant difference in the reported number of sexual partners. Appendix Table 7 (see page 246) shows that both the homosexual and bisexual inmates reported a greater number of sexual partners than did the heterosexual. This fact, of course, is not surprising. What *is* surprising is that over half of the heterosexual sample (55%) *also* reported having engaged in male sex in this prison. It should be pointed out, however, that of these self-defined heterosexual men who reported male sexual activity, three-quarters of them (78%; 68 of 87 men) indicated only minimal sexual contact (as they claimed to have had sex with only one to three different partners). Only about one-quarter of these heterosexuals (22%) claimed they had had male sex with four or more partners. What our study indicates, therefore, is that while heterosexual men are more likely than not *to* engage in male sex in prison, these men are still not as likely to be as sexually active as both the homosexual and bisexual men.

For the most part, number of sexual partners equated with extent or frequency of sexual activity. Some heterosexual men who reported fewer sexual partners, however, were more frequent in their sexual activity, particularly if they were hooked-up. For others, sexual activity involved infrequent encounters with several or many different inmates.

The respondents were also asked the number of times they had *been orally copulated* since coming to this prison. For the total sample, slightly more than half of the respondents (52%) reported having been passive in fellatio. Appendix Table 8 (see page 246) shows the frequencies for this type of sexual activity by inmate's sexual orientation.

For the heterosexual sample, 44% of the men reported having received fellatio since coming to this prison. For those men who had engaged in this sexual activity, slightly more than half had participated only minimally (on from one to three occasions). There were some self-defined heterosexual men (30%), however, who had received fellatio on more than ten occasions.

For the bisexual sample, all the men reported having received fellatio; this was the most active of the three groups. For the homosexual sample, the majority (57%) reported having been orally copulated. However, many homosexuals (43%) reported *not* having been orally copulated. This of course supports our argument that the homosexual in prison tends to play more an active than a passive role in oral copulation. This is due either to personal sexual preference or, more often the case, to his lack of opportunities in prison for sexual reciprocation since he is hooked up with a jocker. (We will say more about this pattern in the chapter on the sexual behavior of the homosexuals.)

Based on the results of our study, it appears that the bisexual inmate is the most active in receiving fellatio, although both a majority of heterosexual and homosexual inmates also reported receiving fellatio.

The respondents were also asked the number of times

they *had performed anal intercourse* on another inmate since coming to this prison. The majority of inmates reported they had *not* participated in this sexual activity, although seventy-seven men (38.5%) did report having performed anal intercourse. Of these men, thirty (15%) reported one to three such encounters; ten reported four to six encounters; one reported seven to nine encounters; twenty-five reported ten to twenty encounters; and eleven reported more than twenty encounters.

By looking specifically at these sexual patterns and comparing them by the inmates' sexual orientation, as Appendix Table 9 (page 247) shows, we can see that the bisexual group is the most sexually active in performing anal penetration. Only 29% of the heterosexual group and 43% of the homosexual group reported having performed anal intercourse. All of the bisexual group (100%), on the other hand, indicated engaging in this sexual activity.

Once again, for those self-defined heterosexuals who had performed anal penetration the majority (57%) had done so only on one to three occasions. There were, however, some heterosexuals (28%) who were quite active in this form of sexual behavior. Furthermore the bisexual group reported having performed anal penetration more often than either the heterosexuals who were sexually active or the homosexuals. All but one of the bisexuals reported having engaged in anal sex on ten or more occasions, and 41% claimed they had performed anal sex more than twenty times.

The respondents were also asked the number of times they had *performed fellatio* on another inmate since coming to this prison. Only one-fifth of our total sample reported having performed fellatio. When we compare the data by the inmates' sexual orientation, as Appendix Table 10 (page 248) illustrates, we can see that the majority of men who performed fellatio are the homosexuals (as we would expect). As the table indicates, only 6% of the heterosexual sample reported engaging in fellatio compared to 59% of the bisexual group and 90% of the homosexuals. These findings once again support our earlier statements regarding the nature of the sexual role played by the homosexuals.

Likewise, in response to the question concerning the number of times the inmates had *been anally penetrated*, the homosexual group nearly unanimously (95%) had engaged in this behavior compared to only 36% of the bisexual sample and 8% of the heterosexual sample. The vast majority of the total sample reported *not* having been the passive partner in anal sex (80%). Of those (primarily homosexual) men who had been anally penetrated, approximately half of them had engaged in this sexual activity on fewer than ten occasions and half had done so more than ten times. Only a few (6% of the total sample) reported having been anally penetrated more than fifty times. See Appendix Table 11 (page 249) for the complete statistics on this sexual behavior pattern.

The results of these above four questions demonstrate the sexual patterns that we have spelled out in the earlier portions of this book where we discussed the effects of the convict prison and sexual code. As the summary in Appendix Table 12 (page 250) points out, over half of the heterosexual respondents (55%) and all of the bisexual and homosexual respondents reported having engaged in some form of male sexual activity since coming to this prison. The form that this sexual activity took depended on their own sexual orientation (except for the cases where forced sexual encounters took place).

The men who defined themselves as bisexuals were twice as likely to report being orally copulated as either the homosexuals or the heterosexuals who reported engaging in sex. Further, the bisexuals were twice as likely as the homosexuals, and three times as likely as the heterosexuals who engaged in sex, to report having performed anal penetration.

The heterosexual men who reported sexual involvement were more likely to "pitch" than to "catch" as they reported a higher incidence of receiving fellatio or being active in anal sex. The bisexual respondent also indicated a higher incidence of sexual activity that would be considered as "masculine" according to the inmate prison code. Only the homosexual respondents reported a higher incidence of being the "feminine" partner in sexual activity. That is, the vast majority (over 90%) of the homosexual respondents reported having performed oral copulation and reported having been anally penetrated. (We will say more about the sexual practices of the homosexuals in prison in a later chapter.)

Based on the responses to these questions (and others to be discussed shortly), there appear to be substantial differences in the sexual patterns of the men who were sexually active in prison. These differences can be ascribed in part to differences in the inmates' sexual orientation. The question arises, however, whether or not some other variable, such as the *marital status* of the heterosexual inmate or the opportunity for the married heterosexual to receive family visitations (and thereby *conjugal privileges*) might be mitigating factors accounting for differences within categories.

According to the data collected, married heterosexuals were just as likely as single heterosexuals, and more likely than separated or divorced heterosexuals, to claim involvement in prison sexual behavior (see Appendix, Table 13).

Further, as Appendix Table 14 (see page 251) shows, married heterosexuals who received conjugal privileges were in fact the *most* likely to report sexual involvement with male inmates compared to those married men who did not participate in the family visitation program (statistically significant at the .05 level). On occasion, in the visiting day room the two men hooked up in prison would individually be visiting with their respective families while at the same time keeping an eye on the other's activities, all of which were hidden from the inmates' families.

The fact that the married heterosexuals were just as likely to be sexually active in prison was a surprising finding since prison administrators and prison reform groups alike have traditionally argued that opportunities for conjugal visits are a means of resolving inmate sexual tension. Based on the results of our study, such visitation privileges (that is, the forty-hour trailer visits) did not seem to have a major impact on the situation one way or another. This might, of course, be due to the fact that married inmates are limited to only four such visits per year. Further, we have no way of knowing the impact on sexual behavior in prison if more frequent conjugal visits were allowed.

Other background and demographic information were also analyzed to see if any characteristic—such as age, term, type of offense, or length of time served—had any bearing on the inmates' sexual activity. None of these variables proved predictive in defining sexual behavior. That is, there was no significant finding linking any of these characteristics with inmates' sexual functioning in prison.

What did explain differences, however, besides the inmates' sexual orientation, was the ethnic or racial background of the convict. These differences were significant, and so we now turn to a discussion of ethnic identity and its impact on inmate sexual behavior.

RACIAL AND ETHNIC CONSIDERATIONS

As countless researchers have noted, any discussion of social and sexual roles and scripts within prison must derive from an understanding of the black ghetto[10] and Mexican-American barrio[11] cultures as they exist outside prison (the importation model). Since blacks and Mexican-Americans comprised close to 60% of the population of this prison, they have virtually dictated the values, norms, and roles within the walls. Similar patterns appear to exist in other penal institutions throughout the state.

Because we were interested in seeing whether or not racial or ethnic identity differentiated the sexual behavior of the heterosexuals, bisexuals, and homosexuals, the data were analyzed looking, first, as Appendix Table 15 shows (see page 251), at ethnic differences and patterns of sexual behavior for the heterosexuals. As predicted, there were significant differences between the black, Mexican-American, and white heterosexuals in reported *number of sexual partners, type* of sexual activity (e.g., reported being orally copulated, performing anal penetration, performing oral copulation, or being anally penetrated), and *frequency* of such activity.

As to actual sexual activity, both the black and Mexican-American heterosexual were much more likely to have engaged in male sex than was the white heterosexual. In fact twice as many black heterosexuals (81%) were sexually active in prison compared to white heterosexuals (38%); over half (55%) of the Chicano heterosexuals were sexually active. These ethnic differences for heterosexuals who were sexually active were a statistically significant finding (at the .0001 level). Based on the results of our study, four-fifths of the black heterosexuals, half of the Mexican-American heterosexuals, and one-third of the white heterosexuals were sexually active in prison; and all of the bisexuals and homosexuals were active.

As the summary in Appendix Table 15 further shows, the black heterosexuals (62%) and Chicano heterosexuals (52%) were more likely to have received fellatio; blacks, in fact, were twice as likely as white heterosexuals to have received fellatio.

The black studs were also twice as likely as the whites to have performed anal penetration, although the frequency for this sexual behavior was not as high as that of receiving fellatio. In both of these dominant and "masculine" sexual roles the black heterosexuals were the most sexually active, with Chicanos and whites following in descending order.

Only in reported number of submissive sexual roles (either active in fellatio or passive in anal intercourse) did the white heterosexuals report a higher incidence than did the black or Chicano heterosexuals. This finding represents one of two patterns: (1) the white heterosexual appears to be less rigid in his sexual role-playing in that he more likely both "pitches" and "catches"; and (2) some of the white heterosexuals who reported "passive" sexual activity had (likely) been forced into this punk role.

The varied incidences of sexual activity reported by these three ethnic groups is due to the fact that for blacks, and to a lesser degree for Chicanos, sex with males is condoned so long as dominance is maintained.

It appears that blacks in prison are quite sexually active regardless of their sexual orientation. Such activity might be explained in this way. Within the lower-class ghetto culture it can be conjectured that sexual promiscuity is more or less tolerated (if not expected), and pimping and hustling are accepted institutionalized scripts. A number of young blacks identify with the "pimp" role and act out the appropriate script. Carried over into prison, the resulting influence is a greater tolerance for promiscuity within defined scripts which translates into both less possessive attitudes regarding sexual monogamy and greater acceptance of both selling sex and paying for it.

In prison it is quite common for one black convict to approach another convict who is the dominant member of the pair and offer to pay him to have sex with his punk (either sissy or kid). Thus black homosexuals are prone to hustle and black convicts are more prone to pay for sex. Material compensation is considered sufficient justification for engaging in sex outside of a relationship as long as both partners agree.

The Catholic-influenced barrio subculture is quite different in this respect. In the Mexican-American culture there is a distinction between prostitutes and "nice girls," or the kind one marries. Mexican men place a high value on their partner's monogamy, and they are extremely possessive and chauvinistic. These scripts carried over into the prison scene result in extremely possessive, dominating relationships. Further, Mexican-Americans will not "turn out" one of their own ethnic group because it is the ultimate insult to "rob a man of his manhood." But if a Chicano youngster *is* a homosexual, he is considered a "broad" or woman and accepted and used within that script.

The case of "Jimmy" illustrates such Chicano "prison social etiquette." Jimmy, a young white homosexual, was transferred to this prison from a maximum-security institution where he had been hooked up with a Chicano named "Tony." After arriving at this prison, Jimmy wanted to hook up with another Chicano named "Joe." Before Joe would hook up with Jimmy, however, they wrote to Tony at the other prison to ask permission. Had they hooked up without Tony's permission, Tony could have put out a gang contract on both Joe and Jimmy for violating Tony's relationship with Jimmy. Jimmy "belonged" to Tony. This is a very rigid code of conduct, and far different from the "looser" black scripts and behavior.

With respect to the white inmates, there does not seem to be any clearly defined cultural script. As the results of our prison sexual survey will show, the white subculture does not accept homosexuality in prison to any great

degree. Some lower-class whites tend to adopt a chauvinistic, possessive stance toward their punks, and the middle-
class whites tend to be more accommodating and less rigid
within their relationships, but the great majority of white
convicts (more so than blacks and Chicanos) avoid involvement in prison sex altogether.

Among these ethnic groups within the prison environment there is some merging and mingling of the various cultural perspectives and scripts. Ethnic and cultural
differences are more a matter of emphasis than absolutes.

Earlier studies[12] have focused on the racial imbalances
in prison rape, with most rapes having black aggressors
and white victims. In our research, while a majority of
rapes follow this pattern of blacks as aggressors and whites
as victims (see Chaper 6), the general sexual pairings are
*not* interracial. Interracial pairings are uncommon in the
prison setting we studied, and almost nonexistent at other
(maximum-security) institutions. The reasons for this taboo
include the strong racial solidarity that the prison gangs
maintain.

As we have noted, it is rare for ethnic minorities to
"turn out" one of their own although they will "get down"
(have sex) with one of their own race or ethnic group who
is homosexual. Both blacks and Chicanos, however, will
turn out a white boy if they get the chance. In one nine-
month period for one quad of 600 inmates there were
seven rapes which were officially documented in disciplinary writeups, but these statistics are deceptive since most
rapes go unreported for fear of individual or gang reprisal.

OTHER ETHNIC DIFFERENCES

Returning to a discussion of the findings from our random sample of the general prison population, the 200
respondents were asked whether or not they had been
involved in an ongoing sexual relationship with another

inmate since coming to this prison. One-fourth of the inmates indicated that they had been hooked up, and this varied by the inmate's sexual orientation and ethnicity. Whereas all the homosexuals in the random sample reported having been hooked up (100%), only 59% of the bisexuals and 10% of the heterosexuals reported this pattern. This was a statistically significant finding in that the inmates' sexual orientation was indicative of whether they were likely to be hooked up or not.

Of the heterosexuals who had been hooked up, both the black and the Mexican-American inmates reported a higher rate than did the white heterosexuals. In fact 17% of the black and 16% of the Chicano heterosexuals reported having been hooked up compared to only 3% of the white heterosexuals. Once again this supports our observation that for the heterosexual in prison ethnicity plays an important role in determining who participates in male sexual activity.

Ethnic differences were also noted for the bisexuals in being hooked up while in prison. Over three-quarters of the black bisexuals (78%), half of the white bisexuals (50%), and one-third of the Mexican-American bisexuals (33%) reported having been hooked up.

Ethnic differences also best explain the differences in responses to several other questions in our study. These included whether or not the inmate was currently hooked up, the number of male sexual experiences he had engaged in prior to incarceration, and his age at first sexual encounter with another male.

Close to one-fifth of the total sample group (19%) reported that they were currently involved in a relationship or hooked up. This was similar to the pattern of responses to the previous question in that more blacks than whites or Mexican-Americans reported that they were now involved in an ongoing relationship with another inmate.

A question was asked concerning whether or not the

inmates had engaged in male sexual activity *prior* to coming to prison. Nearly half of the total respondents (99 of 200) reported that they had experienced prior sexual activity with another male, although these experiences varied by the inmate's sexual orientation. That is, over 90% of both the homosexuals and bisexuals reported prior male sexual activity, whereas only one-third of the heterosexuals (38%) reported prior experiences. This latter figure is comparable to the percentage of men in society at large who have had a prior homosexual experience.[13]

Our findings delineate two interesting patterns: It appears that not all of the homosexuals in prison had had prior male sexual experiences, which means that some of these men "came out" (or assumed a homosexual identity) while in prison. Likewise, it appears that more heterosexual men reported prior male sexual experiences (62%) than reported male sexual experiences while in prison (55%). These "prior" experiences quite likely referred to homosexual acts these men had engaged in while they were much younger. Now that these men were older, they apparently did not have an inclination to pursue homosexual activity in prison.

For those heterosexual men who reported prior male sexual experiences, racial or ethnic differences were again noted. For example, nearly two-thirds of the black heterosexuals (62%) reported prior sexual experiences with males compared to less than one-third of the white (30%) and less than one-fourth of the Chicano heterosexuals (23%). The black heterosexuals had more than twice the number of sexual experiences with males prior to incarceration than had either the white or the Mexican-American heterosexuals. Once again cultural and ethnic patterns formulated prior to incarceration have been imported and replicated inside prison, accounting for major ethnic differences in terms of sexual behavior.

The respondents were also asked at what age they had

had their first sexual experience with another male. Over two-thirds of the total sample (68%) had had some sexual involvement with another male: 13% were under age thirteen when they had their first male sexual experience, 27% were in their early teens, 13% were in their late teens, 8% were in their early twenties, and 7% of the men in the total sample were twenty-five years of age or older before they had their first male sexual experience.

In terms of sexual orientation, both the homosexuals and bisexuals reported same-sex experiences at an earlier age than did the heterosexuals. For example, approximately 80% of the bisexuals and homosexuals reported having had male sexual experiences prior to age seventeen whereas only 48% of the heterosexuals who claimed to have had male sex reported their first encounter at this age. The heterosexual group who reported having participated in male sex had done so at a later age; in fact 15% of these men reported that they were over twenty-five before they had their first male sexual encounter.

Racial and ethnic differences were again noted for this heterosexual group. Both the black and white heterosexuals reported earlier first male sexual encounters than did the Mexican-American heterosexuals. Thus both the bisexual and homosexual group reported earlier male sexual encounters compared to those of the heterosexual group who had been sexually active with another male; and the black and white heterosexuals were younger than the Chicano heterosexuals when they first experienced a homosexual act.

## THE BISEXUALS IN PRISON

Ethnic differences also best explain the varied sexual patterns of the 11% of the men in our random prison sample who reported that they were bisexual.

This group of bisexual men was slightly older (average age was thirty-one) than the average age (twenty-nine) of the men for the entire sample, and the age range for the bisexual respondents extended from twenty-two to forty-four. Nine of the bisexuals were black, ten were white, and three were Mexican-American. Compared to the ethnic breakdown for the total sample, there was a higher representation of blacks in this category.

As to type of offense, seven of the bisexual men had been incarcerated for robbery; the remainder were sent to prison on various other charges. Only one bisexual was sent to prison on sexual misconduct charges. All but five of the men were serving their first term. With respect to their marital status, fourteen of the men reported being single, four were married, three were separated, and one had been divorced.

All the bisexuals in the sample reported having engaged in sex in this prison. Although they did not claim as many different sexual partners as did the homosexuals, the bisexuals were quite sexually active with the average number of different partners being six. Furthermore, over one-fourth (27%) of the bisexuals reported having had from ten to twenty different sexual partners in prison.

Ethnic differences were again apparent in the types of sexual activity the bisexuals experienced. As Appendix Table 16 (page 252) shows, black bisexuals were more likely to have engaged in only the dominant sexual roles while the white and Mexican-American bisexuals indicated more varied sexual behavior. For example, the bisexuals reported a higher incidence of receiving fellatio than did the heterosexuals and homosexuals. Nearly all of the bisexual group (95%) claimed they had received fellatio on ten or more occasions, whereas only one-fourth of the homosexuals (29%) and one-fourth of the sexually active heterosexuals (29%) claimed a similar number of incidents.

In fact two of the bisexual inmates reported having been orally copulated over 100 times.

Whereas ethnic differences will be apparent in terms of the "feminine" or submissive sexual acts, ethnicity did not distinguish the bisexual group in terms of receiving fellatio. The black, Chicano, and white bisexual were each as likely to engage in this sexual activity. Likewise, ethnicity did not explain any differences in being active in anal intercourse. As Appendix Table 12 shows, all the bisexual respondents reported being active in this sexual act. Once again the bisexuals indicated a greater frequency of performing anal penetration than did the sexually active heterosexuals or the homosexuals. As Appendix Table 9 illustrates, 41% of the bisexuals claimed they had performed anal penetration more than twenty times (with one inmate indicating he had performed more that 100 acts of anal intercourse).

The responses regarding performing oral copulation on another inmate, however, did show significant differences based on ethnicity. As Appendix Table 16 shows, those blacks who defined themselves as bisexual were still likely to play *only* the traditional masculine role. Whereas black bisexuals engaged in the dominant roles of receiving fellatio and performing anal penetration, very few reversed the sexual roles. Only 22% of the black bisexuals, for example, reported performing oral copulation compared to 67% of the Mexican-American and 90% of the white bisexuals.

Obviously, in sexual role-playing a bisexual identity has different cultural meanings to this group of blacks than it does to the other bisexuals. For these blacks, to be bisexual means to have sex with other males while still maintaining a traditional, dominant sexual role. For whites, on the other hand, to be bisexual means to be able to reverse sexual roles, to both "pitch" and "catch." In this regard the black bisexual and the black heterosexual jocker are very similar in their actual sexual behavior. The only basic difference appears to be the inmate's own self-definition of his sexual behavior. For some blacks, having sex with another male but maintaining a dominant role warrants a self-identification as bisexual; other blacks engaging in the same behavior still define themselves as heterosexual. For some whites, however, being bisexual not only means engaging in sex with both males and females, but also reciprocating sexually with the male sexual partner.

Ethnic differences were even more pronounced among those bisexuals who received anal penetration. Not one of the black bisexuals reported he had been penetrated. Most of the white bisexuals (70%), however, did report having been involved in this activity. [We are not discussing the Mexican-American bisexuals as the number of respondents in this category (1) is too small to warrant any validity.]

For those bisexuals who did report having performed fellatio or having been anally penetrated, the number of such incidents ranged from one to fifty times. There was a significantly higher reported incidence of performing fellatio than of being passive in anal penetration.

It is quite clear that inmates who claim a "bisexual" identity are influenced by ethnic and cultural considerations. Although the bisexual reported the highest incidence of being the "active" partner in male sex in terms of traditional sexual roles, the black bisexual did not switch roles and perform the passive role to the degree that the white bisexual exchanged sexual roles. Further, bisexuals, regardless of race, who assumed the "passive" role reported a lower incidence of this activity than of playing the "active" role. These bisexual men appeared to be more "comfortable" in playing the traditional masculine role, and although some bisexual men both "pitch" and "catch," most bisexuals in this prison prefer to "pitch." Only four of the twenty-two bisexuals (three whites and one black) indicated that they had been pressured into having sex against their wills, and three of the four stated that this had occurred on just one occasion.

Nearly two-thirds (thirteen) of the bisexuals reported that they had been involved in an ongoing sexual relationship with another inmate, with an average duration of one year. Furthermore, two bisexual men indicated having been in relationships lasting more than two years. Ethnicity also played a role here. Three-quarters (78%) of the black bisexuals stated that they had been hooked up whereas only half of the white bisexuals and one-third of the Mexican-American bisexuals claimed they had been hooked up. Ten of the twenty-two men reported that they were currently hooked up.

All but one of the bisexuals indicated that they had had sexual experiences prior to prison (although one bisexual indicated that he had had only one such prior experience). As to the actual number of prior male sexual experiences, most of the bisexuals claimed an average of eight prior contacts, although two bisexuals claimed 100 prior involvements. Their average age when they first experienced male sex was fourteen. The one bisexual who indicated no prior male sexual experiences before incarceration stated that he was thirty-six before he first engaged in male sex.

## IMPLICATIONS OF THE FINDINGS

By examining the results of this portion of our study, and by looking specifically at the inmates' own sexual orientation as well as the ethnic and cultural differences involved, we have been able to gain a clearer understanding of the sexual dynamics as they exist in this prison. Although we have not yet reported in detail the data for the homosexual group (this will be the focus of Chapter 7), we can state for points of comparison that for the most part the homosexuals play clearly defined sexual roles—in their case, the so-called submissive or "feminine" roles. That is, the homosexuals predominantly are either active in performing fellatio or passive in anal intercourse.

For the bisexual group, and for the group of heterosexual men who had been pressured into sex against their will (to be discussed in a later chapter), the sexual patterns are less clear-cut. As we have shown, the bisexuals generally play the "masculine" role, although this pattern holds true more for the black bisexuals than it does for the white bisexuals. The actual sexual practices of the heterosexual men who have been pressured are more diverse due to the forced nature of the encounters.

As has been noted, the patterns for the black sexually active heterosexuals and black bisexuals are similar. These jockers maintain a dominant, aggressive role and often are the manipulators in prison sexual exploitation. According to the associate superintendent, their behavior appears to replicate the role of pimp that was played outside prison; the only difference is that in prison the effeminate homosexuals and kids comprise their "stable," whereas on the outside females (often forced into prostitution) comprise their stable.

It appears that for those inmates who wish to engage in sex in prison there are ample opportunities in this institution to do so. Since two-thirds of our total prison sample reported having engaged in some type of sexual activity, it appears that sex is condoned by both the convict prison code as well as (tacitly) by the prison administration. The actual sexual practices and patterns that evolve in this environment, however, are strongly shaped by the different attitudes toward male sexuality held by the black, Chicano, and white heterosexual, bisexual, and homosexual inmates; and by the policies of the prison administration (to be discussed in later chapters).

Part II elaborates further on the prison sexual scene. Continuing our discussion on the heterosexual and bisexual inmates who are sexually active in prison and who, because of their dominance, maintain and shape the convict sexual code, we first focus on the male relationships that develop in prison between the jockers and their homosexual partners and punks. We then look in greater detail at the situation of those heterosexual youngsters who are "turned out" in prison, their coping strategies, and experiences in prison. Finally, we expound on the sexual behavior of the self-defined homosexuals, differentiating between the "effeminate" homosexuals or sissies who make up the majority, and the other "types" of homosexuals found in prison.

# II

## THE JOCKERS, PUNKS, AND SISSIES

# Male Sexual Relationships

The various scenarios involved in sexual encounters and relationships within the prison setting are as diverse and individualistic as those on the streets. As we mentioned in the preceding chapter, one overriding factor within the prison setting is the deemphasis of affection and emotional involvement as opposed to physical and sexual considerations. Whereas sexual and physical relationships are condoned within the convict code, emotional or affectional attachments are seen as a sign of weakness. The irony is that in this hard, emotionally cold, and even hostile environment, everyone is starved for affection, although no one would ever admit to it. Furthermore any two people who are able to "find each other" and develop a mutually fulfilling or affectionate relationship would create a great deal of resentment, jealousy, and open hostility. Among this immature, unstable population, that kind of hostility could lead to trouble.

On occasion emotional attachments do evolve and congenial relationships do develop. Although any show of affection is very covert and the projected public front is that of a very casual detached role, the pairs spend a great deal of time together. Other couples, on the other hand,

are seldom if ever seen in public together. It is individualistic, just as it is on the streets.

In the prison under study no one racial group or gang
was in control. According to some of the respondents, at
some of the maximum-security prisons (where they had
served time before being transferred) the gangs to a degree
determine who is to have access to the punks and homosexuals. Within the medium-security prison, and among
the younger generation of convicts, this pattern of dominating allocation of sexual partners is gradually diminish-
ing. In the prison we studied, for example, there is no one
"kingpin" or "Godfather," nor is there a "convict committee administration" in charge which establishes the sexual
relationships. In this prison the sexual pairings are left up
to the two individuals involved, who are free from outside
inmate interference. Once in a while some bully may try
to break in or interfere for his own selfish purposes, but
this is rare since the "man" of the pair is expected to take
whatever steps are necessary to deal with the intrusive
situation.

## ESTABLISHMENT OF RELATIONSHIPS

We discussed before how *casual* sexual encounters
occur in prison. The process in which long-term and steady
relationships develop is quite different and is the focus of
this chapter.

When a new arrival is assigned to permanent housing
and moves onto his assigned tier, he is the "new man" or
"new meat." It is usually at this point that the real "con
games" and pressure start. Very soon thereafter any homosexual or kid new to the tier will usually make a choice and
hook up, if he has not already done so. (In the next chapter
we discuss how the kids or punks are socialized and intim-

idated into the sexually receptive role.) The approaches to these new "fish" are as varied as the individuals involved. Most straight convicts will usually try to run a game dubbed "I want to be your friend." Other convicts will make a more direct, verbal approach, such as in the following case example.

## "Everett"

Everett is about fifty years old and has been in prison for sixteen years for first-degree murder. He is about six feet three inches tall, weighs around 195 pounds, is masculine in appearance, and can be described as distinguished looking, mature, and articulate. Everett claimed never to have had sex with another male prior to coming to prison. Everett works in a technical job with a certain amount of prestige and clout.

Everett stated that he has always kept a kid since coming to prison. When one kid leaves (is discharged from prison), he picks up another one. He is aware of the new arrivals, and when he sees one who catches his eye, he makes a very direct verbal proposition. This proposition, as described by Everett, goes as follows:

Here's what I can do for you, kid, and here's what I want from you in return. I'll provide you with the commissary you want, some drugs [pot], and I'll look out for you, and keep the heat off of you. In return I want you to suck my cock, and occasionally I'll fuck you. You are, also, to follow the rules that I lay down, and stay away from the people I tell you to stay away from.

From our observations, it appears that there is no pressure or intimidation involved. Everett uses a straightforward, honest, no-nonsense approach. Everett states he is sensitive and wise, and "cares" about the kid. In this way Everett is easier to like and treats his kids very well. Everett does not care if his partner is homosexual or heterosexual.

He is always hopeful that an emotional relationship might develop, although he is perceptive enough to accept a relationship on a basis of mutual physical need and not to force affection if it does not materialize. If the person agrees, Everett will seek to arrange (with the guards) for the kid to be transferred to his tier and the relationship will develop from there.

From our observations, Everett and his kid are always in each other's company, except when Everett is working. We get the impression that Everett keeps pretty tight reins. The staff, as we note in Chapter 10, are well aware of what is happening, but they feel that the kid is better off being under Everett's guidance than being "up for grabs" by the "wolves."

Since most of these "straight" convicts do not "catch," they expect the kid one-sidedly to assume the passive role in sexual activity. On occasion a (usually older) homosexual convict will financially support (play the role of a "sugar daddy" to) a good-looking kid or homosexual who then plays the *active* sexual role. Further, a good-looking youngster—either heterosexual or homosexual—who has had experience hustling on the streets, or who becomes a "hustler" (by selling sex for money or other forms of reimbursement), can make out quite well in prison provided he plays his cards right. There is always the danger, however, that someone will take what they want by force. Most inmates who hustle have some sort of "backup" or protection behind them.

The following personal account is that of a young, white homosexual in prison on grand theft charges who discusses his prison sexual indoctrination:

*"Bob"*

When I first arrived, I was approached in a casual, friendly manner by a muscled, young [age twenty-four] black lifer. "Ed" came up to me one day while I was sitting out in the yard. He was friendly and said that he had asked another inmate, who I knew, who was gay, about me. Ed was easy to talk with and pleasant and attractive to me. I was very afraid to get involved with blacks though. Throughout county jail I had been told to stay away from blacks and to respect the racial barriers. Ed was sincere and we talked on several occasions. I liked him. Ed wanted to hook up with me, but I refused because of the racial problems which I felt would result. I discussed this with him at length, and he assured me that here it was much more relaxed than at most joints, and that we would have no problems. I was afraid that the whites would stick [knife] me if I got involved with a black. Since then I have gotten down with Ed on a few occasions. But we never hooked up because of my unfounded fears. Apparently this is the only joint where whites and blacks can be together.

During my first two months here I did have several encounters with various inmates on my tier. I was very cautious though, and selective of who I chose, and turned down many propositions. I was never threatened or heavily pressured by anyone. I am not particularly physically dominant, but I am strong-willed and certainly no passive pushover. I had made up my mind while in county jail that I was not going to be anyone's punk or allow anyone to force me into sex if I could prevent it. When I did finally hook up, it was of my own choosing, and a mutual relationship was formed based on respect and affection. Were I at any joint other than this one, I probably would not have been able to accomplish this. I would have been forced into a dependent relationship. Even here I am quite lucky to have achieved the type of relationship that I have accomplished.

Bob said in his interview that his partner is jealous and to some degree possessive. He indicated that, out of respect for his partner's feelings, he is not particularly promiscuous and stated that "Our relationship means more to me than the cheap thrills of the cruising game."

One difficulty involved in prison relationships is the time element. Overriding any pairing is the divergent time factor between the parties involved. In the relationship referred to above, one inmate is being paroled in ten months and the other is a lifer and has not yet been given a parole date.

Bob also stated that loneliness was not a factor for him

mainly because of his relationship. Apart from his partner he does not have many real close friends, although he has many acquaintances. He contends that loneliness is not much of a factor in general and that most of the inmates form some friendships and socialize within their cliques. Most inmates, heterosexual and homosexual alike, find a "buddy" (or "road dog" as the white bikers call a friend) to socialize and stick together with. As far as homesickness or longing for friends or family members on the outside, Bob stated that this is more common among inmates with wives and children than it is for the single men.

Both Everett and Bob were inmates who were better educated and who could more clearly articulate their sexual experiences and feelings. Most convict relationships, on the other hand, are comprised of inmates from lower socioeconomic backgrounds, who are less educated and thereby less reflective and observant concerning the dynamics of their prison experience. In these other, more typical prison relationships, the nature of the relationship is marked by greater degrees of manipulation and (singular or mutual) exploitation.

## CASE STUDIES OF FOUR "PAIRS"

One aspect of our prison study involved conducting interviews with four typical "pairs" (or couples) of inmates who had settled into a steady sexual relationship. What distinguishes these *sets* of interviews from the preceding accounts is the fact that we were able to interview separately both partners in the relationship. By presenting their respective comments side by side, we can see more clearly the nature (and exploitive dimension) of these typical prison paired relationships.

Two of the interviews were conducted with black pairs and two were with white couples. The two black pairs were typical of the types of relationships found in this prison. Even though these relationships were less rigid and chauvinistic than those relationships that existed, according to the inmates, in the higher security prisons, the distinction continued to be drawn between the dominant partner and the homosexual partner.

The other two pairs discussed in this chapter represent somewhat atypical types of relationships. In the first relationship between the two white inmates, "Tim" and "Curtis," Tim is a typical average gay male while Curtis appears to be a young man who is still "in the closet" and who has not yet "come out" as a homosexual. In the case of "Herb" and "Chuckie," Herb is a low-rider (biker) type who is obviously hustling Chuckie, an effeminate homosexual who appears to be a dependent masochist.

It will be readily apparent from the following four sets of interviews that the atmosphere in prison is not conducive to the development of positive, mutually supportive relationships. (The question of whether or not more positive types of relationships should be allowed to develop in prison at all will be discussed in later chapters.) As we elaborated in the last chapter, the black inmates tend to be looser and more accepting of the whole sexual scene than the whites.

Because the interviews give such a vivid, descriptive account of the dynamics of their relationships, we present the transcripts in their entirety, along with a summary of the background information of each of these eight respondents. (Note that while the jockers of each pair refer to their partners as "she," only males are involved.)

## "Brian" and "Monay"

"Brian" is a forty-year-old black man who was sent to prison for armed robbery and has served five years of his six-year term. This is his second prison term and he is separated from his wife. Brian considers himself to be heterosexual. He states that he masturbates twice a week, has had sexual experiences in this prison with approximately fifteen different inmates, has been orally copulated approximately 100 times, and has performed anal intercourse on another inmate approximately seventy-five times. Brian does not "catch," so he has neither orally copulated another inmate nor has he allowed anal intercourse to be performed on him.

Brian also indicated that he has never been pressured into having sex with another inmate against his will, nor has he been physically assaulted while in prison. He stated that he had engaged in sexual activities outside of prison with other males on approximately twelve occasions, and that he was twenty-four years of age when he had his first sexual experience with another male.

Q: Where were you raised?
A: I grew up in Fresno.
Q: Have you ever been hooked up with anyone other than Monay?
A: Yeah, when I was at Folsom I was hooked up with this broad named "Rae" for about a year, before I got sent here.
Q: How long have you been here?
A: About two years.
Q: How long have you and Monay been hooked up?
A: Since she got here. It's been about eighteen months or so.
Q: How often do you and Monay get it on?
A: About three or four times a week since she moved onto my tier. Before that, maybe once a week or whenever we could.
Q: What do you do sexually?
A: Boy, you're sure asking the questions. I don't know if I should be telling you all this. [He was assured that the information would be kept anonymous.] Yeah, I know it's cool. What was the question again?
Q: What do you do sexually?
A: Well, everything, I guess. She sucks my dick but usually we bone.
Q: Do you kiss her?
A: Hell, yes, we mug.
Q: Does she get off?

*A:* Sometimes she does.

*Q:* Do you love Monay?

*A:* I don't know if I would call it love. I really dig her, though.

*Q:* Does she ever get it on with other dudes?

*A:* Yeah, if they pay her.

*Q:* Do you ever set her up with anyone?

*A:* Yeah, sometimes I do.

*Q:* What if she doesn't want to?

*A:* I don't make her do it. I don't play that shit.

*Q:* Do you ever get it on with anyone else?

*A:* Hell, yes.

*Q:* Does Monay care?

*A:* No, not really. I give her her share.

*Q:* Do you and Monay get along well? Do you ever fight?

*A:* Do you mean, do I hit her?

*Q:* Well, that, or do you argue?

*A:* There ain't no arguing 'cause what I say goes. That's just the way it is. I've slapped her a couple of times when she gets out of line, but it don't happen that often.

*Q:* When you get out, do you think that you'll ever get down with a homosexual?

*A:* Sure, why not? Usually I'm messing with broads though. I've fucked punks on the streets before.

"Monay" is a black inmate, twenty-two years of age, and was sent to prison for two years for theft. Monay has served eighteen months of his sentence. This is his first prison term. Monay had his first sexual experience with another male at twelve and "came out" at fourteen. Monay stated he had had sexual experiences with fifteen different persons since coming to prison. He does not "pitch" but only "catches," having orally copulated other inmates some seventy times and admits to having had anal intercourse performed on him approximately fifty times. He states that he has twice been pressured into having sex against his will, but he has never been physically assaulted he; however has received disciplinary writeups ("115s") for sexual conduct.

In response to several questions concerning his sexual

identity, Monay considered himself to be a homosexual and more feminine than masculine; he did not indicate wishing to be more masculine, to be straight, or to be a female. He appears to be happy and satisfied with his sexual identity.

Q: Where were you brought up?
A: I was born in San Rafael, but we moved to San Francisco when I was about fourteen.
Q: Where were you in county jail?
A: San Francisco.
Q: Did you have any sexual experiences there?
A: Yes, there was this brother in my cell and we would do it. I was sort of hooked up with him while I was there.
Q: Did he pressure you, or did you do it because you wanted to?
A: I did it because I wanted to.
Q: How about at Chino?
A: I wasn't at Chino. I went through the reception center at Vacaville.
Q: Did you have any sexual experiences while you were there?
A: Yes, I did it with a few of the dudes on my tier.
Q: Were you pressured?
A: Sometimes, but I wasn't really forced, just bothered a lot.
Q: Then you wanted to do it?
A: Not really. Sometimes I did. This one dude came into my cell and kept insisting that I suck his thing, and he wouldn't leave so I just did it. But I wasn't really forced or anything.
Q: How long have you and Brian been together?
A: Ever since I got here.
Q: Do you love Brian?
A: Yeah, I sort of love him.
Q: How often do you and Brian have sex?
A: About three times a week.
Q: Where do you usually do it?
A: In his room, because he has a lower bunk, but sometimes in mine. [There is only one bunk to a room, but the rooms share an adjoining wall and bunks are staggered one on top and one below, to conserve space; see Figure 1 on page 27.]
Q: Have you ever been busted by the guards?
A: Yes, Brian and me have been caught twice, and I was caught with some other guys.
Q: Tell me what happened?

*A:* Well, the first time, "Mack" [a guard] caught Brian and me, but he didn't write us up. He just gave us some extra duty. The other time "Bill" caught us and he wrote us up.

*Q:* Did he catch you in the act?

*A:* Not quite, but Brian was in his shorts and I was naked on the bed. He wrote it up as a "compromising position."

*Q:* What happened?

*A:* We got five evenings lockdown. [After receiving a "115," there is a hearing before a lieutenant who decides whether or not the inmate is guilty and issues a punishment. Lockdown means being locked or confined to one's room except for meals.]

*Q:* Tell me about the time he caught you with the other guys.

*A:* Mack caught me in "Jim's" room with him and "Bloomer."

*Q:* You mean that you were having a "three-way"?

*A:* Yes, Brian was supposed to be pointing. [Jim and Bloomer were paying Monay and Brian a carton of cigarettes apiece for Monay's services.]

*Q:* How come Brian let Mack come up on you?

*A:* Well, he was down at the other end of the hall, and Mack came through the back door and was looking in the windows [the small five-by eight-inch windows in the solid doors to the rooms].

*Q:* Did he catch you in the act?

*A:* Yeah, he sure did. Jim and Bloomer had been drinking "pruno" [wine made from yeast stolen from the kitchen and mixed with sugar, water, and available fruit; it is mixed in large plastic garbage-liners and hidden in the inmates' cells]. When they saw Mack at the window, Jim dived for his pants and fell off of the bed onto the floor.

*Q:* Did Mack write you up?

*A:* He sure did. I got ten days lockdown, and Jim and Bloomer got seven evenings because it was their first time.

*Q:* What do you and Brian usually do sexually?

*A:* Whatever he wants to do.

*Q:* Does he reciprocate?

*A:* Not really.

*Q:* Do you get off?

*A:* I do when he fucks me.

*Q:* Does Brian get down with other homosexuals?

*A:* Yeah, once in a while.

*Q:* Does it bother you?

*A:* Not really.

*Q:* Has Brian ever hit you?

A: He slapped me a couple of times, but he doesn't ever really hit me or anything.

Q: Do you think that homosexuals have it harder in prison than straight convicts?

A: Yeah, not so much here as at other places. It all depends on how you handle it.

### "Ed" and "Flo"

"Ed" is a typical black bisexual jocker. Now twenty-four, he has served six years of a life sentence for first-degree murder. This was his first offense and he has never been married. Ed reports masturbating three times a week. Since being in prison he has had sexual experiences with twelve different persons and has been orally copulated approximately 150 times and has performed anal intercourse over 200 times. He stated that he has never orally copulated another inmate nor has he had anal intercourse performed on him. He also has never been pressured into having sex nor has he been physically assaulted. Ed stated that outside prison he engaged in sexual activities with other males on approximately eight occasions, and that he was fifteen years old when he had his first sexual experience with another male. Ed considers himself to be heterosexual.

Q: Where did you grow up?

A: Watts, California.

Q: Have you been hooked up with anybody prior to Flo?

A: Yes, while I was at Chino I was hooked-up with a homosexual named "Terri."

Q: How long were you hooked up?

A: For about six months.

Q: How often did you guys have sex?

A: She lived on another tier so it was hard to get together. We had to sneak, so we could only get together maybe once every week.

Q: What did you do sexually?

A: I would fuck her.

*Q:* Did she give you head?

*A:* No, I don't get off on head. I like to fuck.

*Q:* How long have you been here?

*A:* Two and a half years.

*Q:* How long have you been hooked up with Flo?

*A:* About two years.

*Q:* Do you love her?

*A:* Not really. I like her a lot. I'm not sure I even know what love really is.

*Q:* Does she love you?

*A:* I don't know. Ask her.

*Q:* What do you and Flo do sexually?

*A:* I fuck her. I told you, that's my thing.

*Q:* How do you fuck her? What position?

*A:* I like it best with her on her stomach. Sometimes we do it "family style" [missionary position] or she sits on my dick.

*Q:* Do you kiss her?

*A:* Ah, when we're fucking.

*Q:* Does she get off?

*A:* She usually jacks off while I'm fucking her.

*Q:* Does Flo get it on with other guys?

*A:* Well, it depends on who it is.

*Q:* What do you mean?

*A:* If I don't like them or something, then I don't go for it.

*Q:* You mean that you have to approve of who she does it with?

*A:* Yeah, I'm looking out for her. If she gets into trouble, I'm the guy who has to take up the slack.

*Q:* You don't get jealous?

*A:* No, I don't get jealous. Why should I?

*Q:* What if she started liking someone else and wanted to hook up with him?

*A:* That's her choice to make. I ain't forcing nothing on her.

*Q:* What if some other dude tried to pressure her?

*A:* If anybody disrespects her, it's just like disrespecting me. I'll talk to the dude first, and if that don't get things straightened out, then we'll get down. ["Get down" as used here refers to the use of fists, shanks (knives), or whatever is necessary to establish dominance.]

*Q:* Has that ever happened?

*A:* No, not really. Everyone around here knows that she's hooked up with me. Ain't nobody going to fuck with her.

*Q:* How well do you get along? Do you fight or argue much?

*A:* We get along pretty good. She does what I say.

*Q:* Have you ever hit her?

*A:* No, but I might if she really fucked up or something. I don't believe in hitting broads, or punks.

*Q:* Do you ever set her up with someone else?

*A:* No, I don't pimp her or anything like that.

*Q:* Do you ever get it on with anyone else?

*A:* Sure, if I want to.

*Q:* How often?

*A:* Whenever it happens. Sometimes more often than others; it all depends on what's happening at the time.

*Q:* Does Flo care?

*A:* I don't care whether she does or not. I do what I want to do.

*Q:* Do you think that you'll get down with homosexuals on the street?

*A:* You mean fuck punks? Sure, that's some of the best pussy there is.

"Flo" is a typical effeminate black prison homosexual. At twenty-four he has served three years of a seven-year sentence for second-degree murder. This is his first offense. Flo stated that he had his first sexual experience with another male at eleven and that he decided he was a homosexual at thirteen. Flo has had sexual experiences with fifteen different persons since coming to prison.

Flo has played both active and passive roles in sexual activity, although he predominantly "catches." He claimed to have orally copulated other inmates approximately 100 times and has had anal intercourse performed on him some 150 times. He stated that he has been pressured into sex on three occasions but that he has never been physically assaulted. Flo has received two disciplinary writeups for sexual conduct. Flo defines himself as a homosexual, and claims he is more feminine than masculine.

*Q:* Where did you grow up?

*A:* Pomona.

*Q:* Where were you in county jail?

*A:* Los Angeles "Old County" [Los Angeles has two jail facilities, new and old county].

*Q:* Did you have any sexual experiences in county jail?

*A:* No, I was in the "Queen's Tank" [Los Angeles has a special segregated unit called the "Queen's Tank" for effeminate homosexuals].

*Q:* How many of you were in the tank?

*A:* About twenty.

*Q:* How about at Chino?

*A:* I got it on about three or four times. It was hard to do because they kept me in a single cell.

*Q:* Were you pressured?

*A:* No.

*Q:* You wanted to get it on with the dudes you had sex with?

*A:* Sure. There was one guy who worked as a medical assistant who used to call me into the hospital and we would go into this room and do it.

*Q:* What did you do?

*A:* Once he fucked me standing up. Well, I mean, I bent over, but mostly I sucked him.

*Q:* Where did you get the name Flo?

*A:* My brother started calling me that when I was about fourteen. My real name is Floyd.

*Q:* Why did he call you Flo?

*A:* Because I was a sissy. I used to like to dress up in my sister's clothes and jewelry. I used to get it on with my brother, too.

*Q:* How old were you?

*A:* Oh, about thirteen the first time.

*Q:* How old was he?

*A:* He was sixteen or seventeen.

*Q:* What would you do with your brother?

*A:* Suck his dick and he would fuck me.

*Q:* How long did this go on?

*A:* About two years, until he went into the army.

*Q:* Were you doing it with anyone else?

*A:* Yes, I used to do it with a couple of his friends, and some of the other boys around the neighborhood.

*Q:* Tell me about the three times you were pressured into having sex since you have been here in prison.

*A:* It happened the first time when I was on fish row. This dude came into my room and he pulled out his cock and it was hard and he wanted me to suck it, so I just did it.

*Q:* You didn't want to?

*A:* No, he was a real asshole, and I didn't like him. He had been bothering me for several days. I just did it to get him out of my room.

*Q:* What about the other times?

*A:* Well, I was new on the tier, you know, and I didn't know anyone and all these assholes kept fucking with me, so a couple of times I did it just to get rid of them. But then I started doing it with this one brother, and he kept everyone else away.

*Q:* Were you hooked up with him?

*A:* Sort of, but not really. He was "short" [close to release]. Then I met Ed and hooked up with him.

*Q:* How long have you and Ed been together?

*A:* Over two years.

*Q:* How often do you guys get together?

*A:* You mean, get down?

*Q:* Yes, have sex.

*A:* Oh, about twice a week, sometimes more.

*Q:* Have you ever been caught by "the man"?

*A:* I was caught in Ed's room once, but we weren't doing nothing.

*Q:* Did you get a 115?

*A:* No, it was "Carl" who caught us and he just warned us.

*Q:* What do you and Ed usually do sexually?

*A:* He fucks me.

*Q:* Does he kiss you?

*A:* Yeah.

*Q:* Do you get off when you're having sex?

*A:* I usually get off when he fucks me.

*Q:* Do you ever get down with other guys?

*A:* Sometimes, not too much.

*Q:* Have you ever gotten down with another homosexual?

*A:* No sissies, but a couple of times I've gotten it on with a dude and we've "flip-flopped" [exchanged sexual roles].

*Q:* Was he gay?

*A:* Yes, but not a sissy—sort of undercover, you know.

*Q:* How about Ed? Does he ever do it with anyone else?

*A:* Yeah, a few times he has.

*Q:* How do you feel about that?

*A:* It makes me jealous.

*Q:* Do you guys fight much?

*A:* No, sometimes we do though. I mean, we argue sometimes. He's never hit me.

*Q:* Does he support you?

*A:* No, well, if he's going to the store and I need something, he'll get it for me, but I do the same for him.

Q: Do you feel that homosexuals have it harder in prison than straights?
A: In some ways they do. You know, the homosexuals are always being fucked with.
Q: You mean for sex?
A: Yeah, but when you're hooked up it's not so bad.
Q: How would you describe your and Ed's relationship?
A: I don't know. I really dig Ed a lot. He treats me good. We have a good understanding, I guess. I don't know. What can I say?

## "Curtis" and "Tim"

"Curtis" is a twenty-three-year-old white inmate who has served two years of a three-year sentence for vehicular manslaughter. This is his first offense. He is divorced. Curtis stated that he masturbates twice a week. Since coming to prison he has had sex with two different persons. He has been orally copulated approximately twenty-five times and has performed anal intercourse some thirty times. Curtis stated that he does not "catch." He also indicated that he had engaged in sexual activities with other males outside prison on four occasions. He was fifteen when he had his first sexual experience with another male, and he considers himself to be bisexual.

Q: Where did you grow up?
A: From the time I was about twelve, in a small town in Louisiana.
Q: Where were you arrested?
A: In San Diego, California. I was in the marines stationed at Camp Pendleton.
Q: Have you ever been hooked up with anyone besides Tim?
A: Tim and me aren't really hooked up. We're just sort of good friends, you know. I just sort of look out for him.
Q: You guys do get it on sometimes, don't you?
A: Yeah, but it's no big thing.
Q: How long have you guys been together?
A: About a year and a half.
Q: How often do you have sex with Tim?
A: Whenever it happens. There's no set schedule.
Q: About how often?

*A:* Oh, I'd say maybe once or sometimes twice a week. Maybe not at all, it just depends.

*Q:* What do you guys usually do when you do it?

*A:* What do you think? I don't know. I mean I don't do nothing to him. I mean maybe I bone him, or he gives me some head, but I don't fuck around with him.

*Q:* Do you ever kiss Tim?

*A:* Fuck no! I ain't into that shit.

*Q:* Does Tim get off?

*A:* No, well sometimes he jacks off. This is kind of weird. I mean, I really ain't into talking about this kinda shit. It's really nobody's business. [Tim was reassured and the reasons for the interview were reexplained.]

*Q:* Have you ever got it on with anybody besides Tim?

*A:* Yeah, I got a "header" once from this homosexual on my tier, but that was before I met Tim.

*Q:* Does Tim get down with anyone else?

*A:* No, not that I know of.

*Q:* Would you care?

*A:* What Tim does is his business, just as long as he stays cool. I just sort of keep the heat off of him. You know, when he first got here a lot of dudes were pressuring him.

*Q:* On the questionnaire you described yourself as bisexual?

*A:* Yeah, well I get down with a dude so I must be bisexual.

*Q:* Do you think that you'll get down with dudes once you get out?

*A:* I don't know. It sort of depends on how it comes down.

*Q:* Do you and Tim get along well? Do you argue or fight much?

*A:* Once in a while we get pissed at each other, but nothing really serious. He's a good kid. We get along pretty good.

*Q:* Tell me about your experiences with dudes before you came to prison?

*A:* Well, it was just kid stuff. You know, jacking-off together and playing around.

*Q:* Did you ever have any sexual experiences with dudes while you were in the marines?

*A:* Yeah, once in San Diego this dude picked me up hitchhiking and he smoked a good joint with me, and we got to rapping and he seemed like an alright dude. So he asked me if I wanted to go over to his pad and get loaded. He had a big pad on the beach in La Jolla and we smoked a lot of weed and drank beers, and I crashed there. In the middle of the night I woke up and he was sucking my dick. It

felt good, so I thought "What the fuck!" I guess I sort of expected it
to happen.

Q: Did you ever go back to his house?

A: Yeah, once, but I didn't stay long. Nothing happened.

"Tim" is a twenty-one-year-old Caucasian who has
served sixteen months of a four-year sentence for sales of
dangerous drugs. This is his first offense. Tim was ten
when he had his first sexual experience with another male
and he was eighteen when he came out as a homosexual.
Since coming to prison Tim has had sexual experiences
with eight different persons. He has been orally copulated
approximately fifteen times and he has performed anal
intercourse on another inmate on two occasions. He has
orally copulated another inmate some thirty times and has
had anal intercourse performed on him some twenty times.
He indicated that he had been pressured into having sex
on two occasions, but he was never assaulted nor has he
received disciplinary writeups for sexual activity. Tim
identifies himself as both a homosexual and a bisexual. He
considers himself to be masculine, he would rather not be
straight, and he is happy with his current sexual identity.

Q: Where were you raised?

A: I was born in Downey, but we moved to Laguna when I was thirteen.

Q: Where were you in county jail?

A: San Bernadino County.

Q: Did you have any sexual experiences there?

A: No, I was only in there about two days and then I got bailed out.

Q: You were out on bail while fighting your case?

A: Yeah, it took about nine months. I thought I was going to get off with
county time, but the judge gave me four years.

Q: How about at Chino? Did you have any sexual experiences there?

A: Chino was the pits. God, that place is fucked. I was really scared. The
guy I was in a cell with was in for murder. He started driving on
me the first night. He threatened to beat me up. He could have done
it, too. He was about six feet three inches tall. I was really afraid of
him so I gave him what he wanted. Well, what he really wanted
was to screw me, but I said that I couldn't take it, so I sucked him

off. He transferred out two days later and the next guy they put in with me was all right. Then I got a job in the chow hall after about a week and I moved down to where the workers stayed. I met this guy down there that I had met at county jail and he sort of looked out for me. I got moved into his cell. His name was "Glen" and he was a real nice guy. I did it with him a lot.

Q: What would you do?

A: Either I'd suck him off or sometimes he would screw me. I got it on with some of the other guys who worked in the chow hall, but I just gave them blowjobs.

Q: What happened when you got here?

A: Well, when I first got here, one of the guys from Chino who knew I was gay was on fish row with me and he told everyone that I was gay so everyone was driving on me. The guys would just push their way into my room and demand blowjobs.

Q: Did you do it?

A: What else could I do? With some of them I didn't mind, but a lot of them were real creeps.

Q: Were these whites or blacks?

A: Mainly blacks, but a couple of them were white.

Q: Did any of them fuck you?

A: Yes, I'd usually try to give them blowjobs, but sometimes they forced me to let them screw me.

Q: By forced, do you mean that they physically assaulted you, or just threatened you?

A: Yeah, they would threaten me. A couple of times they would grab me and push me around and I would give in. Usually there were two of them. One would watch out for the other one and then they would switch.

Q: Did they hurt you?

A: You mean when we were having sex?

Q: Yes.

A: Well, they weren't easy, but at least I made them use grease.

Q: How long did this go on?

A: While I was on fish row, about three weeks.

Q: Then what happened?

A: I was sent to A Quad, and I met Curtis.

Q: How did you and Curtis come to hook up?

A: He lived on my tier and when I moved on he was the only one who was friendly to me. At first I thought he might be gay because of the way he sort of cruised me. Well, one time we were in the shower together and he got a hard-on and then so did I. So after we got out, he came down to my room with just his towel on and we had sex.

Q: How often do you guys usually do it?

A: At least twice a week.

Q: What do you do sexually?

A: Everything. Whatever we feel like doing.

Q: How do you get off?

A: Curt usually jacks me off.

Q: Curt jacks you off, is that all?

A: Well, sometimes when he's really horny he blows me, but he won't let me come in his mouth. Don't tell anyone that I told you this. Curt would kill me.

Q: Have you ever fucked Curt?

A: Well, I really shouldn't say anything, but twice he let me screw him. The first time he asked me to do it.

Q: Did he like it?

A: He says it hurt, but once we got into it he liked it. I know he did because he came while I was screwing him.

Q: Do you think Curt is gay?

A: Well, I think he's coming out, but he won't admit it to himself. He's kind of hung up about it. He can't accept it yet.

Q: Do you talk to him about it?

A: Not really. He doesn't like to talk about it.

Q: How would you describe your relationship? Do you love each other?

A: Gosh, I don't really know how to answer that. I love Curt, I could really love him if he would let it happen. He has feelings for me, I know, because sometimes they show through. We have a good relationship. We spend all of our time together.

Q: Does he kiss you?

A: A few times when we've been stoned and he's screwing me, he kissed me.

Q: Do you feel that homosexuals have a harder time in prison than straight inmates?

A: Absolutely, of course they do. Everybody is trying to get over on them. I think there should be a special quad just for gays so that they wouldn't have to put up with all the games.

## "Herb" and "Chuckie"

"Herb" is a twenty-three-year-old white inmate who has served three years of a four-year term for manslaughter. This is his first offense. Herb is single. He stated that he masturbates three times a week. Since coming to prison Herb has had sexual experiences with four different persons. He claimed to have been orally copulated approximately fifty times and to have performed anal intercourse around thirty times. Herb does not "catch." He indicated that he had no prior male sexual experiences before coming to prison. He considers himself to be heterosexual.

Q: Where were you brought up?
A: San Clemente.
Q: Is Chuckie the first person that you've been hooked up with?
A: Yes, but I've fucked around with a lot of punks before.
Q: Here in this prison?
A: Yes, and when I was in Y.A. [Youth Authority]. There was this one punk called "Flipper" that I used to fuck with all the time.
Q: How long were you in Y.A.?
A: Altogether about four years. I was in twice.
Q: How old were you?
A: I was fifteen the first time I was sent there. I was in for about eighteen months.
Q: Have you played around here much?
A: A few times. There was this one punk who used to live on this tier and she would suck our dicks in the TV room late at night after everyone had gone to bed.
Q: Who's us?
A: Me and "Mike" [Mike is Herb's best friend or "road dog"]. We never fucked her though. That bitch was uglier than shit. I used to just close my eyes and pretend it was a real broad.
Q: How long have you and Chuckie been hooked up?
A: Since she moved on the tier, over a year.
Q: How often do you get it on with her?
A: Whenever I'm horny. I don't know, about three times a week.
Q: Do you love her?
A: Hell no, I don't love that bitch. I just like to get my rocks off. It beats beating off. That shit gets old.
Q: What do you do sexually?
A: Usually she just sucks my dick. Sometimes I fuck her if I feel like it.
Q: Does Chuckie get off?
A: I don't give a fuck. Once I get off, I split.

*Q:* Where do you usually do it?

*A:* In my room or hers.

*Q:* Does Chuckie get it on with other dudes?

*A:* Only if I tell her to. Sometimes she sucks Mike's dick.

*Q:* Do you ever do it with anyone else?

*A:* I've let that blond punk on the second tier suck my dick a couple of times.

*Q:* Does Chuckie care, or does she know?

*A:* She ain't got nothing to say about it. She don't call no shots.

*Q:* Does Chuckie love you?

*A:* She loves my dick. Hell, I don't care. All I'm interested in is the bread she spends on me.

*Q:* Does she spend a lot of money on you?

*A:* Hell, yes. That bitch has got money. She spends fifty dollars every month on commissary. She bought me some shirts and two brand-new pairs of levis. [Inmates are allowed to wear *only* levi pants. Visitors to the prison *cannot* wear levis so that they can be easily distinguished from the felons.] Whatever I want, she buys me.

*Q:* How do you guys get along? Do you argue or fight much?

*A:* There's no arguing. If she pisses me off, I'll slap that fat bitch in the head.

*Q:* You hit her?

*A:* Fuck, yes, I hit her!

*Q:* Do you hit her very often?

*A:* Not lately. She hasn't been pissing me off.

*Q:* What if Chuckie decided to split from you?

*A:* She won't split. She likes my dick too much.

*Q:* Do you like Chuckie at all?

*A:* I like her all right, for in here. He sure sucks my dick good.

*Q:* Do you think that you'll ever get it on with a punk on the streets?

*A:* I would if he paid me enough.

"Chuckie" is a twenty-four-year-old white who has served eighteen months of a four-year sentence for a drug charge. This is his first sentence. Chuckie had his first male sexual experience at eleven and came out as a homosexual at seventeen. Since coming to this prison Chuckie has had sexual experiences with eight different inmates. Chuckie only "catches" and has orally copulated another inmate some fifty times and has had anal intercourse some twenty-five times. Chuckie claimed he had been pressured into sex on two occasions. He defines himself as homosexual, claims he is equally feminine and masculine, and is satisfied with his sexual identity.

Q: Chuck, where did you grow up?
A: In Tennessee.
Q: Where were you arrested?
A: Los Angeles Airport.
Q: Were you in the Los Angeles County Jail?
A: Only for about twelve hours before I bailed out.
Q: When was your first sexual experience in prison?
A: I made it with a couple of men at Chino.
Q: Did they pressure you into it?
A: They didn't have to, honey, after I saw what they had in the showers.
Q: Tell me about it.
A: Honey, I sucked those big wee-wees. They used to come to my cell when everyone had gone to the gym. They would take turns pointing for each other.
Q: Did you ever get pressured or forced?
A: No, I was always too willing. No, I'm just kidding. A couple of times this nigger that lived in the next cell hassled me so I just did it and got it over with. He sure had a cock on him! It must have been twelve inches.
Q: How about here in this prison?
A: Well, you know "Rick," that lives down on the first tier, right side— the one with all the muscles and blond hair? Well, I had him a couple of times when we were on fish row. He fucked my socks off. I loved every minute of it. God, he's a beautiful man.
Q: How did you hook up with Herb?
A: He started hanging around when I moved into the building, so I got it on with him and he keeps coming back for more.
Q: Do you love him?
A: Are you kidding? I don't love anybody. I just love their cocks. No, I'm just kidding.
Q: Do you get it on with anyone else?
A: No, Herbie gets jealous if I do.
Q: How about Mike?
A: Oh, Mike, he's hot! I've had him four or five times. He's got a beautiful big cock.
Q: How often do you and Herb do it?

*A:* Twice a week. Sometimes twice a day. Sometimes he just can't get enough.

*Q:* What do you do?

*A:* Everything, honey. Whatever he wants to do. This girl's not choosy.

*Q:* Do you and Herb get along well, or do you fight a lot?

*A:* We argue sometimes.

*Q:* Has he ever hit you?

*A:* No, and he better not ever try it. I'll have his ass kicked and he knows it. He knows better than to try that shit on me. I've got too many friends around here.

*Q:* Do you feel that homosexuals are subjected to more abuse in prison than nongay inmates?

*A:* Are we ever! Of course there's a lot of advantages, too. Look at all of the fine men around, honey. We've got a captive audience!

# 6

# The Punks in Prison

Although our discussion to this point has focused primarily on the prison scene as practiced by some heterosexuals and bisexuals and its effect upon the homosexual inmate, incidents of sexual exploitation, intimidation, and assault have also occurred to some of the heterosexual inmates as well. Furthermore, the psychological consequences of these attacks may be far more damaging to those men whose basic sexual orientation is heterosexual, because the victims feel a sense of loss of their "manhood." Moreover, support systems and assistance have not developed in prison to assist these young men with their trauma nearly to the extent that support systems and assistance have developed for their homosexual counterparts, as we discuss in Chapter 11.

In our random prison survey, 9% of the heterosexuals in our sample reported having been sexually assaulted since coming to this prison. Twelve of the fourteen men who had been "turned out" were Caucasian and two were black (no Mexican-American heterosexual reported having been pressured into having sex). In terms of age, the heterosexual men who had been sexually assaulted were younger (average age was twenty-three) compared to the total prison sample (average age was twenty-nine). Like-wise, the range in age for this group of men was narrower (from twenty-one to twenty-six) compared to the age range for the total prison population (twenty to fifty-nine).

As to marital status, eight of the fourteen men indi-cated they were single, five men stated they were married, and one man indicated that he was divorced. Of the five married men, four had received conjugal visits while in prison. Thus even though these men were being pressured sexually and forced to assume the "passive" role in prison, they were apparently maintaining their heterosexual ori-entation with regard to sexual activity with their spouses.

Of these fourteen men who had been pressured into having prison sex against their will, three had each been pressured by only one inmate. At the other extreme, two men reported having been forced into sex by eight differ-ent inmates at different times. Most of the men who had been forced to have sex reported having been victimized by four other inmates. It appears that once these men had been pressured into sex and labeled as a "mark," they con-tinued to be "hit on" by other inmates as well. This pattern also held true for those bisexuals (2%) and homosexuals (41%) who reported having been sexually victimized against their will.

As for actual sexual activity, the heterosexual men who had been pressured reported participating in primar-ily "submissive" sexual roles such as performing fellatio or receiving anal penetration. None of the fourteen men in the random sample indicated that they had been involved in an ongoing relationship, although in our case studies and interviews with "punks" (discussed later in this chap-ter) we did find instances in which the punks were hooked up. Nine of these fourteen men reported some prior male sexual experiences before incarceration. This was similar to the proportion of the total heterosexual sample (64%) that reported prior sexual involvement (though minimal) with other males. For these nine men who reported prior experiences, the average age at their first experience was fourteen; for those five men whose first male sexual experience was in prison, their average age was twenty-one.

## Socialization into Prison Sexual Roles

As we have discussed, any new arrival in prison who projects the image of being young and attractive and/or homosexual will be approached by many individuals in many different ways within a short period of time. These youngsters have usually already been subjected to sexual pressure even before reaching the prison. Most county jails have four-, six-, and eight-man cells for housing felons, and large "tanks" or dormitory-type cells which may hold up to forty bunks housing those men who have committed misdemeanors. These cells are often overcrowded, forcing people to sleep on mattresses on the floors. Sexual pressure in these facilities usually starts out verbally and may increase to rape. However, the psychological stress and insecurity of the jail or prison environment are usually sufficient to render scared youngsters susceptible to verbal manipulations.

On the bus from the county jails and reception centers to prison, the new inmates are dressed in a white cotton outfit with white drawstring pants. At the prison these new "fish" are required to wear their "whites" for the first three days in order to allow the guards to get acquainted with the new inmates and to be able to recognize them. The new inmates stay on "fish row" approximately three to four weeks, segregated on the top floor of one of the buildings. They lockdown behind grill gates at 6:00 P.M. During their stay on fish row they are processed through a state-mandated orientation program whereby they are acquainted with the various programs available in prison and the rules and regulations of the institution, and some are seen by the staff psychologists.

The following excerpt from one of our case studies of kids who were turned out is fairly typical of how these young inmates—either heterosexual or homosexual—are socialized into the prison sexual role of "punk." In many ways this story is no different from that of Barry described at the beginning of this book. For "Jeff," however, sexual pressure began in the county jail before he reached the prison walls.

### "Jeff"

Nineteen-year-old Jeff was booked into Los Angeles County Jail for possession of dangerous drugs. This was his first arrest, and he was an average, scared kid. After the trauma of being arrested and a three-hour booking procedure, he was searched, fingerprinted, researched, photographed, stripped, anus checked, showered, and sprayed for body lice. Then he was given a jail-issue set of clothing and processed through a series of holding tanks and finally assigned to a cell. He was sent to a six-man unit where the other five men had been living in the twelve- by ten-foot cell for two weeks and had formed a social bond. Two of these men were black and in prison for armed robbery, one was Caucasian and in for parole violation, and two were Mexican junkies. Into this setting entered Jeff, bedroll in hand, steel bars slamming shut behind him. He immediately encountered cold stares and, as he related to us, "hard vibes." He was, as the convict saying goes, "a sheep for the wolves."

Lights went out at 9:00 P.M. Jeff was lying on his bunk when one of the black ex-cons moved in and sat on Jeff's bunk and asked, "Hey, kid, you ever been in jail before?

What you in for?" This was just friendly small talk—a big-brother "come on." The words implied security and counsel, but actually they were part of the strategy of the "snake stalking its prey." The next night the same black told Jeff that those other four guys "wanted his ass" and that they were talking about "taking it" that night. The con told Jeff, "What are you going to do? Listen, kid, I can handle them. I can keep them off of you. But I have been in this hold for six weeks and I sure am horny. I sure could use some head. How about tonight after everyone is asleep. You take care of me—no one will know—and I'll look out for you while you're here."

It was the old convict game, the classic play, and each man in the cell played along to make it work. They merely waited for Jeff to take the bait and "cop some rod" and then they "awoke" and demanded their fair share.

Some of the other "kids" interviewed had been approached by a demand similar to the following: "Hey, kid, we want your ass. You can either give it up or we'll take it. It's up to you. You can do it the easy way or the hard way."

The following account was written by a self-proclaimed "dirty old man who happens to be a lifer in a California prison." During our extensive interview he offered to write this paper to better inform us of the critical issues that *all* young Caucasian inmates face as they are processed from county jail into prison. Because it accurately delineates the experiences that many of the "punks" described to us, the paper is reprinted here anonymously and in edited form.

## "Decisions"

Decisions, decisions, decisions! That is the name of the game for a young, good-looking (or even half good-looking) white male coming to a California prison.

The critical period for this youngster is from the minute he reads on the bulletin board in the Guidance Center that he is being transferred to such-and-such a prison, after his six- to eight-week processing. That notice on the bulletin board immediately tells him if he was lucky enough to transfer to a "soft joint" (relatively easy time with a minimal amount of sexual pressure) or to be unfortunate enough to be sent to a "hard joint" (a prison where he will have to literally fight to keep the jackals from making his rectum twice its normal size within one to two days after he steps off the bus at his destination).

Does all of this sound overly dramatic, exaggerated, distorted? It is not meant to be, and it is not. It is called "The Facts of Prison Life for Good-Looking Young Whites." It becomes a "horror" story if he gets transferred to one of the "hard joints" and can be either easy or hard in the "soft joints." The other prisons fall somewhere in between.

The first lesson "Allan" has learned in the Guidance Center is that he is surrounded by a high percentage of horny incarcerated felons with little or no moral values, who are bitter and hostile about a variety of subjects. These felons may be mad about not getting county jail or probation; or they just got a "Dear John" letter or divorce papers from the wife; or they would not be in prison if their crime partner had not testified against them ("ratted on him"), et cetera.

Allan has many propositions thrown his way during his short stay in the Guidance Center. Some are subtle, some not. Some men pretend they want to be his friend; some offer canteen privileges, cigarettes, or some good grass for his body. Some want to fuck him, some want to suck him, some want Allan to suck or fuck them. Some want to make him into a woman by having him pluck his eyebrows, or wear bikini shorts. But, generally speaking, there is no real threat to him—a threat such as being physically beaten up because he would not cooperate, or being raped or having a shank [knife] put to his throat for his sexual favors. To repeat, this is generally speaking, because there are physical assaults, there are rapes (single and gang style), and there are threats with weapons.

But the Guidance Centers are usually closely supervised. There is a train-station atmosphere with people coming and going all the time, and a guy can stay in his cell except for meals and ducats [a pass to go somewhere to take a test or be interviewed].

The second lesson that Allan learns is that all these sex-starved individuals do not seem to pay any attention to the black queens or black homosexuals, nor do they seem to show any interest in the Mexican queens or Mexican homosexuals in the Guidance Center. He soon finds out, also, that all the sex-starved whites are not interested in the blacks [primarily because of the negative peer pressures that would develop in such a situation] and that the Mexican male inmates quickly establish "territory rights" to virtually all of the Mexican gays and Mexican queens. Fully aware of how possessive and "macho" Mexican males are (or appear to be), the white inmates give a wide berth to the Mexican homosexuals.

Then comes the bus trip to the prison where Allan will do most of his time. And now, during the long bus ride, he must make the following decisions:

(1) Is he going to hook up willingly with one guy who will keep everyone else off of him?

(2) Is he going to get into fist fight after fist fight and not submit to sexual demands? Is he so weak that he has no choice?

(3) Which race or ethnic group should he choose to hook up with sexually, or does it matter to him or to the rest of the inmate population? If he is physically strong [good build, healthy], will that hide his mental weakness? Or, conversely, if he is mentally strong, will that overcome his obvious physical passivity?

(4) Will he go directly to "Protective Custody," a single cell in a section of the prison where no one will be able to attack him sexually?

(5) Will he hook up with one person or with a gang? A gang would probably give him much more and better protection, and also would provide him with drugs, but he would then be passed around to different gang members like "a box of Ritz crackers."

(6) Should he hook up with the first decent con who propositions him, one who will treat him as a human being even though Allan will be his "kid" or his "punk"?

(7) Should he attach himself to a guy approximately his own age, or to an older con who has been around for a while and knows all the game-playing tricks other cons will use to entice Allan into becoming their "kid"?

(8) Should Allan look for a con, regardless of age, who makes a full $100 draw a month at the inmate canteen and can supply him with any drugs or other items he wants?

(9) Or should he go with the guy who will treat him as a human being between sexual encounters?

Questions similar to these will bounce around in Allan's head during the bus ride to his new "home" for the next few years. They will also keep him awake at night for the first week or two after he arrives at the new prison. Because Allan is of average intelligence (a good omen), but because he is also a "fish" (a bad omen), there will be many conflicts in his mind in his day-to-day dealings with the sex-starved, psychotic, paranoid, and hostile general inmate population.

The first thing Allan learns in his new "home" is that this general inmate population does not give a damn whether or not he is gay or straight. That comes as quite a shock to him. He asks himself why everyone would expect him to play the game when he is straight. By the same token, a new gay inmate asks himself why everyone expects him to "put out" just because he is homosexual. But Allan, who can be either gay or straight, reluctantly accepts the fact that in prison no one gives a damn what he is sexually. All the mainline cons know is that he is "a good-looking piece of meat" and they want that "meat." And then it *really* sinks into Allan's mind that there is little if any difference between his position if he is gay or straight, since it is his being young and good-looking that is the prized commodity.

Two other questions also plague Allan.

(10) Will he permit sex play from another inmate for "X" number of packs of cigarettes (the same as currency in prison) to "turn a trick"? Allan has to size up his economic situation. Can he expect anyone "on the streets" to send him money to buy the basic necessities like deodorant, toothpaste, soap, and shampoo? Or has Allan any skills that can be used to get a job in the prison with a high pay number (clerk, typist)?

(11) If he hooks up with someone for protection, will he be sold to another convict when his "old man" transfers, paroles, or gets locked up in long-term segregation?

*Every* white youngster coming to prison for the first time must wade his way through this seemingly endless series of questions and then decide what is best for him.

Unless he looks like Dracula.


## Prison Life for the Punks

As we have discussed, it is unusual for either black or Chicano youngsters to be turned out. The blacks and Mexican-Americans tend to look out for their own, and will not turn out one of their own race. Unfortunately, whites do not have the same sense of racial identity and pride. If a white youngster is being pressured by either blacks or Chi-

canos, the other white heterosexuals will use it to their
advantage to turn him out. So white youngsters are preyed
upon by all races. Moreover, whites do not go after black
or Chicano kids because they know that the respective
races of the latter two groups will back up their members.
This pattern accounts for the high incidence of white
youths' being "hit on" in prison. This racial pattern held
true for this prison; in fact, only two black punks could be
identified in prison to be interviewed for our study. The
remainder of the fourteen case studies were conducted
with white youngsters who had been sexually victimized
in this prison.

   Once a kid has made his choice and hooked up, he is
automatically left alone. It is an unwritten code that one
does not mess around with someone else's kid or punk. In
the joint, most kids are accepted as part of the clique that
their old man runs with.

   As we have implied, there are really only two choices
open to these vulnerable youngsters. Either they face on
their own pressure that is overwhelming and constant, or
they hook up with someone who will look out for them.
Occasionally a kid will find someone who is willing to take
the responsibility for him without making any sexual
demands on him, but that situation is rare. Almost everyone in prison, as on the street, is out to get what he can get.
Occasionally if a youngster is tough and "shows heart" he
will gain the respect of the convicts and be left alone.
Again, this is rare.

   The reason a person cannot appeal to the prison
authorities for help is that this would be considered
"snitching." Once someone in prison is labeled by the
inmates with a "snitch jacket" (having gone and com-
plained to the authorities), he is unable to "walk the main
line" (live among the general prison population) for fear
of reprisals. His only alternative is to request protective

custody (P.C.), which means segregation from the total prison population and a total lockdown. Protective custody is not a viable alternative for someone with a lot of time to do since the isolation is psychologically devastating. Being separated from virtually all human contact for the full period of incarceration is a drastic measure, and most inmates would rather "take their chances" of being further sexually victimized than being segregated and alone. Furthermore, once a person "P.C.'s" anywhere in the prison system, it is permanent so that even if the youngster were to be transferred to another penal institution he would have to go immediately into "P.C." since his "snitch label" would, through the inmate rumor system, follow him into the new prison.

Our case studies of these punks indicate that most of those kids coerced into sexual relations in prison remain—at least in their own self-image—heterosexual. Of this group, six of the kids had never had a homosexual experience before being "turned out" in prison, six had had only incidental male sexual experiences in early adolescence, and two had had more extensive homosexual experiences before incarceration even though they continued to identify themselves as heterosexual. Regardless of their prior experiences, none of these kids acted either "homosexual" or "feminine" in prison. Nor did any of them associate or identify with the other prison homosexuals or "queens." Forced to hook up, these youngsters maintained a heterosexual front while engaging in homosexual behaviors. In this respect, it is often quite difficult for the prison staff to identify the punks, although their constant interactions with their "old man" at meals and on the quad give ample clues as to what is really going on.

To further illuminate the effects of punk status on these youngsters, we here include summary reports from three of our case studies and then discuss their common situations in greater detail.

## "Gene"

Gene is a twenty-two-year-old who has been in prison for twenty-six months. He is serving four years for taking part in an armed robbery. Gene is from New Mexico, although he had been unemployed and living in the Porterville, California, area prior to his arrest.

Gene had his first heterosexual experience when he was sixteen, and has had approximately 200 experiences since then. He has gone steady with several girls. Prior to prison Gene's only homosexual encounter was "messing around with a couple of friends when he was twelve or thirteen." From the Guidance Center, Gene was sent to a maximum-security prison where he was heavily pressured sexually by both blacks and whites. At that prison he was cornered in a restroom by two blacks who forced him to perform fellatio. After that time, word got around that he was "available" and he finally had to hook up with a white inmate to keep the pressure off him. During the next year and a half at that prison he was forced to "put out" for six different white inmates who were in his "old man's" clique. At the same time he was having sex several times a week, both oral and anal, with his "partner."

Since transferring to this prison, Gene has been hooked up with three different men. He only has sex now when it is demanded of him. He does not enjoy these sexual encounters, and considers himself to be heterosexual. His experiences over the past two years have seemingly taken their toll. He projects a very defeated outlook and a low self-esteem. Gene is five feet eight inches tall and weighs 140 pounds. He also has a babyface.

*"Mike"*

Mike is twenty-one and has been in prison for eight months. He is serving eighteen months for probation violation (sales of cocaine). He is a high school graduate and worked for a wholesale grower prior to his arrest. Mike is six feet one inch tall and weighs 165 pounds, and is very good-looking.

Mike's first heterosexual experience occurred when he was thirteen and he has had approximately eighty such experiences with about thirty different females. He has also had occasional homosexual encounters with an older brother and three friends which involved both anal intercourse and oral copulation. Mike considers himself to be heterosexual. He has had no contact with the gay scene per se outside prison nor does he like "faggoty-acting" homosexuals.

At Chino Mike was pressured heavily and finally got involved in an incident where he was stabbed in the side with a pencil by an inmate who was attempting to intimidate him into a sexual encounter. After arriving in this prison he was subjected to a great deal of pressure from many inmates, and eventually hooked up with "Bear" to keep the pressure off him. His relationship with Bear is casual and Mike is basically free to do as he pleases. He has sex with Bear about twice a week, usually performing oral copulation. He has had several encounters with "Tommy," a young homosexual who is hooked up with another inmate named "Stan." Stan does not object since both Mike and Tommy are considered "broads" and this is no threat to either Bear's or Stan's position. Mike and Tommy "flip-flop," exchanging sexual roles. As Mike stated to us, "There is no shame in my game." Mike has also been paid for sex on several occasions, both by older homosexuals and by straight convicts. Mike is sexually versatile, which differentiates him from the more predominate types of passive youngsters who are found in prison.

## "Eric"

Eric is a twenty-four-year-old black inmate. He has been in prison for six years and is serving a life sentence for murder. He was reared in Sacramento and dropped out of high school in the tenth grade.

After processing at Chino, Eric was sent to one of the "hard-core" violent institutions, predominantly comprised of inmates under twenty-five who have committed violent crimes or who have violent personalities. Eric, on the other hand, is quiet, soft-spoken, and intelligent; he is not a violent personality. (The prison administrator pointed out that many felons who have committed only one murder offense, as opposed to those who have a life history of many types of criminal activity, often exhibit very calm characteristics and are "ideal" prisoners. This is why they are often subsequently transferred to this prison.)

The murder for which Eric was convicted was committed by his crime partner, but Eric was present when it occurred. Eric was only nineteen when he was first sent to prison. He was gang-raped by six black convicts during his first weeks there. After that, he was hooked up to varying degrees with four different persons. While at the maximum-security institution he was subjected to a great deal of sexual abuse and pressure. Because of the constant strain and tension, he developed an ulcer and received many disciplinary writeups. After four years there he was transferred to this prison. Here he hooked up with an influential black convict who is intelligent and treats him well. Their relationship has evolved into a close friendship with no sex involved. Eric had never had any sexual experiences with males prior to incarceration. He had had only a few prior heterosexual encounters.

## CONSEQUENCES OF THEIR SITUATION

Gaining information from the fourteen punks through interview procedures proved to be extremely difficult, partly due to their embarrassment at being publicly identified and labeled as a punk. Although it was common knowledge in prison that these young men were hooked up, this "knowledge" is seldom discussed openly. If an inmate were to discuss this, the punk's "old man" might take affront.

What is most apparent from both observing and interviewing these youngsters is how their body language indicates defeat and even humiliation. These kids do not project a sense of strength nor do they appear to have a positive self-esteem, a situation that was *not* generally true for the effeminate homosexual group. If anything, these passive youngsters appear to be more often quite distraught because of their sexual victimization even though some of them had been fortunate enough to have developed congenial relationships.

In this prison these punks receive no special program per se. There may be individual counseling on occasion, but they receive no structured, organized, or group-support programs. In part this is due to the difficulty the staff has in publicly identifying (and thereby labeling) these young men. Often they are left to their own coping devices although, as the associate superintendent informed us, the staff does try to get these men to share with them what is happening so as to provide them with some type of assistance.

In this regard the prison scene for these kids is bleaker and more destructive than it is for the homosexuals who are exploited. At least, as we point out in the last chapter, the homosexuals have opportunities for socializing and for religious services, and have organizations external to the prison environment which are attempting to see that the prison system improves its social conditions to lessen the incidence of sexual assault and victimization. Such efforts on behalf of the homosexuals would of course improve prison conditions for the vulnerable heterosexuals as well.

It should also be pointed out that not all of these passive heterosexual youngsters' problems stem from prison sexual victimization. Some of the punks, according to the prison administration, have what might be referred to as "essentially inadequate personalities." That is, some of these punks are provocative victims. They do relatively little to improve their situation but merely passively set themselves up to be victimized. They present an image of weakness and vulnerability, and do nothing to create an image of psychological strength or well-being. In these instances, according to prison officials, the staff tries to counsel them to accept responsibility for their own welfare.

Another type of punk that is identified by the prison administration is the "aggressive manipulator." This type strings jockers out across the yard and often gets two men to fight over him. In effect he is an entrepreneur and uses sex as his payoff. Continuing his role of hustler, he now is using sex as "bait," whereas prior to incarceration his hustling involved nonsexual activities. According to the prison administrator we interviewed, this type of inmate is disrespected by the staff and creates a lot of trouble for the guards since jealousies and fights develop because of his behavior. This type of inmate is also referred to as a "canteen" punk.

While we would concur that these latter two types of punks exist in this prison, the more typical punk was the vulnerable heterosexual youngster who had *not* deliberately set himself up for victimization and exploitation. In fact, none of our interviews was conducted with a punk who appeared to be either the "provocative victim" or the "aggressive manipulator." One interview, however, was conducted with an immature inmate who shared some of these maladaptive characteristics.

*"Randy"*

Randy, twenty-two years old, has served thirty months of his six-year term for armed robbery. A high school dropout, he has lived on his own since the age of sixteen. Randy is six feet, one inch and weighs 145 pounds. He is slim, has long hair, and has the appearance of a "low-rider." Randy's first heterosexual experience was when he was fifteen and he has had many experiences since then. Prior to his arrest he was living with a woman; they were both junkies. Since he was sixteen Randy has on occasion hustled men for money by allowing himself to be orally copulated (used as "trade").

After arriving in this prison, Randy got into debt for $70 through mismanagement of drug transactions and was under threat of violence to repay the debt. "Jones," a very dominant black convict, offered to pay off Randy's debt and take the heat off him if Randy agreed to be his kid. Because of these threats and pressure, Randy hooked up with Jones. Their relationship, however, was constantly volatile due to both Jones's dominance and Randy's immaturity. After four months it ended when Jones brutally beat Randy; as a result, both were placed in isolation and eventually were reassigned to separate quads.

Apart from these isolated types, the majority of punks in prison more closely fit the profile of victims of the prison sexual code. And although we should not lose sight of the fact that these men have committed crimes warranting their incarceration, we should not on the other hand be oblivious to their experiences while in prison. Furthermore, the vast majority of these inmates, at least in this medium-security prison, are short-termers and will therefore be returning to society in the relatively near future.

As we have seen, prison sexual victimization has important ramifications for both the perpetrator and the victim. For the jocker, these sexual "conquests" serve to establish his status and dominance within the convict hierarchy as well as continue to validate his manhood. The use of force becomes conditioned with the sexual act itself (an example of "stimulus generalization"). The men's prison environment allows for, and even sanctions, sexual aggression but does not approve of sexual affection or love except in rare instances; and very seldom does this positive element occur between the "straights who use" and their punks or sissies. Aggression is more commonly used by the jocker to keep the inmate in line. For some, the challenge of turning out a heterosexual youngster is much more exciting than engaging in sex with a willful homosexual sissy who readily appears to conform to the feminized role. Further, since the effeminate homosexual does not resist, opportunities for displacing the jocker's sexual aggression are lessened and thereby the sexual dynamics and release are less satisfying. In this regard both the passive heterosexual and the masculine-defined homosexual (to be discussed in the next chapter) remain "prized objects" since force is required to get them to "fall into line" and assume submissive sexual roles.

Currently there are no sure ways to assess the damage done to individuals who have been sexually victimized in prison. Recent sociological research on men arrested for committing heinous crimes against unsuspecting male hitchhikers and young homosexuals, and research on male hustlers who have subsequently robbed and/or assaulted their homosexual patrons, suggests that the perpetrators of these often brutally sadistic crimes *were themselves* sexually victimized when they were younger, while placed in foster homes or while incarcerated in institutions such as juvenile hall, youth authority, county jail, or prison. As the researchers noted, "With no programs of therapy offered in the nation's institutions for victims of jail rape, it is not suprising that those thus victimized occasionally react in rage towards furtive, frightened, and sometimes insensitive sexual partners."[14]

This pattern implies that for some heterosexual (or severely repressed or marginally homosexual) men, the experience of prior sexual victimization may cause a psychological trauma so severe that opportunities for "revenge" in later life may take the extreme form of (multiple) homicide. Scientific research is needed to further study the long-term psychological effects to men who have been sexually victimized while in custody.

The policy official of the State Department of Corrections, in discussing these patterns, noted that it is not uncommon for a kid who has been turned out as a punk in one prison to, in turn, become a jocker once transferred to another prison. This is a clear example of the victim becoming the victimizer. When questioned as to why this occurs (or is allowed to occur), the official claimed that for these men, this strategy becomes their means of survival. Rather than being victimized by the prison sexual code, they become (if they can) part of the very group that perpetuates the code. Quite likely for some, these learned aggressive patterns during incarceration become coping strategies for life outside prison with, as prior cited studies have shown, potential consequences to the general public.

Since 14% of our prison sample (including 9% of the

young heterosexuals) reported sexual victimization, an alarming number of men are being subjected to an experience which has potential ramifications to society once these men are released. It is paramount that these men be given proper assistance and counseling, if for no other reason to stem the possibility of their becoming future assaulters. Futhermore, it is alarming that these sexual assaults on heterosexual youngsters occurred in a prison which housed homosexuals who in some instances would have willingly engaged in sexual activity.

Although we did not observe these "punks" in a controlled scientific way, we did note that the majority of them held negative self-attitudes. One inmate, for example, mentioned that he was "no good anymore" because he was "less of a man," and that he "was no good to himself or to anyone else." Research shows that heterosexual men who have been sexually victimized outside a prison setting report engaging in compulsive heterosexual activity and/or excessive drinking.[15] These "options" are obviously not available to the prison sexual victim. The effects of sexual victimization in prison appear to be more psychological, as the kids experience depression, anxiety, and even physical symptoms such as ulcers and nausea.

For some of these men it is not the physical act *per se* which is most consequential and damaging, but the fear of being labeled a "queer" or "an easy mark" or "just a punk." Quite likely if men in general were as *casual* with respect to instances of male sexuality as they were with regard to masturbation, they would not react so negatively. Thus the problem for these men appears to be more in the *stigma* attached to the sexual act than in the actual physical experience itself. Although the sexual assault may in some cases cause physical complications and pain (as in the case of women who have been similarly sexually assaulted and raped), the greater damage is psychological. The assault victim—both heterosexual and homosexual—must contend with the fact that he has been physically and psychologically violated. The homosexual, however, is better able to handle the sexual aspect of the act.

Another unique feature to the prison sexual assault is the fact that it parallels the "incest" situation whereby a family member makes sexual advances toward another family member. The prison setting, like the family setting, is a *closed* system. That is, in both instances the victim is living in close proximity with the perpetrator. And often like the family situation, the offender in prison is not held accountable for his actions. Rather it is the *victim* who is punished for the sexual act (either psychologically or punitively). One of our case studies provides an excellent example of this "blaming the victim" pattern when sexual assault has taken place in prison, and demonstrates why so little prison rape is reported by the victim to the prison authorities.

### "Ray"

"Ray" was young, passive, white, and straight, twenty-one years of age, who was still on fish row. One Saturday evening when the majority of inmates were at the movie, two blacks forced their way into his room and raped him. One kept watch while the other raped Ray, and then they switched places. Although they threatened him with reprisals if he told, after they departed Ray went to the guard office in tears, told the lieutenant, and identified his two black assailants.

Ray and his two assailants were all thrown into the "hole"—Ray for protective custody and the two blacks pending their disciplinary hearing and prosecution in the courts. Although they were physically separated in the hole, they were within yelling or talking proximity. While housed in this segregation unit the blacks threatened Ray and told him that if he testified against them, their partners on the outside would retaliate against his family—and Ray got scared. So when the district attorney came to interview Ray concerning filing the charges, Ray suddenly could not make positive identification. Also, at the institutional disciplinary hearing the same thing occurred—Ray was not able to make positive identification. Subsequently the blacks were found to be not guilty, no charges were filed, and they returned to their quad. Ray, in the meantime, was sent to another quad where he was still subjected to the same exploitation, especially now that he had a reputation for having already been "had" once.

This type of procedure, or so it appeared to Ray, was a tactic used by the prison staff to discourage rape proceedings. The staff quite likely knew what was going on in segregation. They knew that Ray was going to be threatened. The staff did not want the "bad publicity" of rape prosecutions within their prison. They did not want the official documentation that this type of behavior was occurring. They preferred, or so it seemed to Ray, to sweep the whole affair "under the rug," pretending that it had not happened.

What can be done about these injustices? (We will address this issue more specifically in the final chapter.) Our prison respondents expressed a strong desire for the staff to segregate the young and passive inmates—both homosexual and the "kids"—who are particularly vulnerable to sexual exploitation and assault. As it now stands, according to the inmates we interviewed, the staff does not seem to be strongly concerned about these matters. Our respondents suggested that all these "potential" victims be assigned to a separate floor of one building which the other inmates are strictly forbidden to enter. This would virtually eliminate all rapes and overtly forced sexual encounters. At the same time those men who were housed on this special wing could still "roam" at their own discretion.

Furthermore, the respondents suggested to us that the most effective strategy for humanizing the plight of these sexual victims in prison is to strive toward further changes in the attitudes of the staff and the Department of Correction's placement policy. All of the respondents concurred that these youngsters should not be placed in potentially volatile situations. (We will say more about the placement procedures in the final chapter.)

This chapter on the fate of the punks has pointed out the fact that sexual violence continues to occur in this prison. In our survey, 9% of the heterosexuals (and 2% of the bisexuals and 41% of the homosexuals) indicated they had been pressured in varying degrees into having sex against their will. Sexual tension remains a reality even in this medium-security prison where conditions are reportedly more favorable than in the maximum-security prisons. The issue of how rehabilitation for inmates can take place in an environment that subjects 14% of its inmates to sexual exploitation remains an issue and concern that needs to be addressed.

# 7

# Behavior and Attitudes of the Homosexuals

Since there is much exploitation of homosexuals in prison, and since the pervasive behavior in prison to some degree is homosexual in nature, we decided to study prison homosexuals in greater detail. Our discussion in Chapter 4 pointed out that self-identified homosexuals comprised slightly over 10% of our total random sample. If we conservatively used this figure as representative of the percentage of homosexuals in prison (a figure that is often used as representative of the percentage of homosexuals in American society as a whole), then 10% of the total prison population of 2400 men would be approximately 240 men who are homosexuals. We were successful in sampling one-third of this estimated total group.

Data for this homosexual sample was gathered in the following fashion (as we outlined in the opening pages of Chapter 1). A forty-two-item questionnaire was distributed to self-admitted homosexuals (see Appendix A for a copy of this questionnaire). The co-researcher personally contacted homosexuals known to him throughout the institution. Other respondents were solicited at a meeting of the

Metropolitan Community Church (MCC), a religious organization that provided services for homosexuals. Because
of the personal contact and solicitation of each individual,
80 responses were received out of 100 questionnaires distributed. This accounted for a response rate of 80%. The
following results reflect the diversity of the homosexual
population in this prison, although we may have underrepresented the very "closeted" homosexuals. In summary,
of the 240 men we estimated to be homosexual in this
prison, 80 men (or one-third of the total homosexual
group) participated in our survey of homosexuals in
prison.

### SURVEY OF BACKGROUND AND ACTIVITY

Background questions were asked of our homosexual
respondents which had also been asked our general prison
population.

The average *age* of our eighty homosexual respondents was twenty-nine, which was also the average age of
our random prison sample. It should be pointed out once
again, however, that the bisexuals in our total prison sample were on the average older (thirty-one) and the heterosexuals who had been turned out in our sample were
on the average younger (twenty-three).

The age range for this homosexual sample varied from
twenty to fifty-one years. By age groupings, nearly one-
third were between twenty and twenty-four, one-quarter
were between twenty-five and twenty-eight, and the
remainder (42%) were twenty-nine or older. Six homosexuals in our sample were over forty years of age.

In terms of *ethnicity*, blacks accounted for 46%, Caucasians for 33%, and Mexican-Americans for 21% of our
homosexual respondents. This sample of eighty homosex-

ual men included a higher proportion of blacks and a lower proportion of whites compared to both the figures for ethnic breakdown for the total prison population (as determined by the Department of Correction's data) and for our random prison sample. The number of Chicanos was proportional to their percentage in prison.

Although our sample is comprised of a larger number of blacks compared to their percentage in the total prison, we do not feel that we have overrepresented black homosexuals in our survey. It appears that this prison held a greater number of overt ("outfront") black homosexuals. And because many of these black homosexuals were effeminate, as we shall show, the "homosexual scene" as it existed in this prison was largely defined by this ethnic group.

This was also true to a lesser degree for the Mexican-American homosexuals. As previously stated, the prison sexual code, jointly shaped by the cultural patterns of the blacks and Chicanos, contains certain expectations for homosexuals. And it is the black and Mexican-American homosexuals, already socialized into these behavioral patterns, who continue to adopt the code (e.g., feminine behavioral patterns) and who largely define the homosexual scene as it exists, or is allowed to exist, in prison. The whites (regardless of their sexual orientation) are forced to accept this code. Although there are some exceptions to this pattern (which we present in the next chapter), the primary role for homosexuals in prison is to adopt "feminine" ways and assume a "submissive" sexual role.

As to the *nature of the offense* that sent these men to prison, a higher proportion of homosexuals indicated having been arrested on drug charges compared to the total prison population (15% versus 6%). Likewise, homosexuals were more likely to have been sent to prison on charges of burglary (21% versus 13%) and theft other than auto theft

(9% versus 3%). Further, homosexuals were *less* likely to have been sent to prison for more violent crimes such as committing homicide (13% versus 22%). In the other categories there was no significant difference between the homosexual sample and the total prison statistics.

It appears that the homosexuals were sent to prison for lesser offenses. In fact, burglary (21%) and drugs (15%) accounted for over one-third of the offenses that sent these men to prison. Only one respondent of these eighty homosexuals stated that he was sent to prison on a sexual misconduct charge.

With respect to the *number of terms* these men had served, the homosexual group did not differ significantly from our total prison sample. For both groups approximately two-thirds of the respondents were serving their first prison term.

Our homosexual respondents were asked at what age they had had their *first sexual experience* with another male. Their responses ranged from five to twenty-five years of age. The median age was thirteen and a half.

The respondents were also asked at what age they had decided they were homosexual (or "come out"). Their responses ranged from ten to thirty years of age. The median age for "coming out" was seventeen and a half. By comparing these two median ages, it appears that there was a time-lag on the average of four years between the time they first experienced a male sexual encounter and when they assumed a homosexual identity. This time interval for the "coming out" process is also documented in the social science literature for the homosexual population in society as a whole.[16] In those studies, however, the age at "coming out" ranged from the late teens to the early twenties. Our prison population, it appears, assumed homosexual identities earlier than homosexuals studied in non-prison settings.

There were no significant differences between the

blacks, whites, and Mexican-Americans in either the age at which they had their first male sexual experience or the age at which they assumed a homosexual identity.

SEXUAL EXPERIENCES IN PRISON

The homosexual sample was asked questions similar to those asked the random prison sample with respect to their sexual experiences since coming to prison this term. Only summary patterns will be discussed in this chapter. (See Appendix A for a copy of the questionnaire.)

All eighty men in our homosexual sample indicated that they had been sexually active since coming to prison. In terms of actual number of sexual partners, their responses ranged from one to upward of 100. The majority of homosexuals claimed that they had had sex with from ten to twenty different partners.

This figure varied significantly from the number of sexual partners reported by our random prison sample (see Chapter 4). In the total sample, most of the inmates who reported sexual activity claimed same-sex contact with only one to three different inmates. And although the bisexuals were more sexually active than the heterosexuals who engaged in male sex, neither of these two groups matched the high levels of sexual activity reported by the homosexuals. Not only were the homosexuals more sexually active, they were also active with a greater number of sexual partners.

As to *type of sexual activity,* as expected the homosexuals reported higher incidences of performing oral copulation and being anally penetrated than receiving oral copulation and performing anal penetration. These patterns, however, were particularly true for those homosexuals who defined themselves as "feminine," as we discuss in greater detail below.

In terms of *being orally copulated,* less than half (49%)

indicated that they had received fellatio. Those who had been orally copulated reported having engaged in this activity from ten to twenty times. When their responses are considered by ethnic group the Caucasian homosexuals reported the highest percentage (62%). Both the white and black homosexuals, furthermore, were twice as likely to have received fellatio as were the Mexican-American homosexuals. Appendix Table 17 shows the differences for the ethnic groups with respect to the distinctive patterns of sexual behavior for the homosexuals (see page 252).

The homosexuals were also asked about the number of times they had *performed anal intercourse* on another inmate. Less than half (41%) reported that they had engaged in this activity although they did not report frequent involvement in this sexual act. Only a few men (9%) reported performing anal intercourse over a half a dozen times. As we have noted, the homosexuals are restricted in terms of their "type" of sexual activity.

Ethnic differences were again noted. Both the black and white homosexuals were twice as likely to report having performed anal intercourse as were the Mexican-American homosexuals. As Table 17 shows, black homosexuals were the most likely to have engaged in this sexual activity.

Nearly all of the homosexuals (95%) reported having *performed oral copulation*. Some of these men, in fact, were quite active—14% reported having performed fellatio over 150 times. Interestingly, there were *no* significant ethnic differences in frequency of performing fellatio. Black, white, and Chicano homosexuals were equally sexually active in this type of sexual behavior.

Again, nearly all of the homosexuals (98%) reported having *been anally penetrated*. Furthermore the actual number of incidents was quite high; nearly half (43%) of the men reported they had been anally penetrated on over fifty occasions. In fact 10% reported being passive in anal sex over 150 times.

As with the previous question, no significant ethnic differences were noted. All three ethnic groups participated equally in being anally penetrated. As Appendix Table 17 shows, being passive in anal sex was the most common sexual activity engaged in by the homosexuals. That is, homosexuals in prison were more likely to have been anally penetrated than they were to have performed oral copulation, to have performed anal intercourse, or to have received fellatio. Furthermore, the homosexuals were twice as likely to have played a "feminine" role than to have played a "masculine" role in prison.

The respondents were also asked to identify to what degree they considered themselves to be *more feminine* than masculine. In terms of sexual behavior, the feminine-defined homosexulas reported a significantly higher incidence of having been anally penetrated (see Appendix Table 18; see page 253). Although the feminine-defined homosexuals reported more frequent passivity in anal penetration compared to the masculine-defined homosexual, no differences were reported by the two groups regarding participation in fellatio. That is, the masculine-defined homosexuals were just as likely to have performed oral sex as were the femine-defined homosexuals. Thus the more feminine homosexuals performed both submissive sexual roles whereas the more masculine homosexuals were more likely to have performed fellatio than they were to have been anally penetrated.

The issue of sexual exploitation was central to our study, so three questions were asked pertaining to this issue. One question asked the respondents about the number of times they had *been sexually harassed*. Nearly two-thirds (64%) reported having received some type of sexual pressure (either verbal or physical). In fact, thirty five of the homosexuals (44%) claimed they had been pressured one to three times, thirteen (16%) claimed four to six times, and three (4%) claimed they had been pressured seven to nine times.

Interestingly, the feminine-defined homosexuals were no more likely to have received sexual pressure than were the masculine-defined homosexuals. The data showed no indication that the presentation of a feminine identity would make the homosexual any more vulnerable to sexual exploitation.

Differences were noted, however, in terms of ethnic identity. White homosexuals, irrespective of their feminine or masculine projection, were the most likely to have been pressured into sex. Over four-fifths of the white homosexuals (82%) claimed they had been pressured compared to slightly more than two-thirds of the Mexican-American homosexuals (71%) and less than half of the black homosexuals (49%). Furthermore, over one-third of the white homosexuals (35%) claimed they had been pressured into sex on repeated occasions (four or more times). By comparison, nearly two-thirds of the Chicano homosexuals (65%) and one-third of the black homosexuals (32%) claimed sexual pressure on fewer occasions (one to three times). The white homosexuals, as expected, were more likely to have received sexual pressure and to have been pressured more often than either the Chicano or black homosexuals.

In fact it was the more masculine-defined homosexuals who reported higher rates of physical (although not necessarily sexual) abuse. The respondents were asked about the number of times they had actually *been physically assaulted* by another inmate. One-third of the men (34%) reported having been physically abused. Twenty-three homosexuals (29%) claimed they had been physically assaulted one to three times, and four (5%) claimed they had been attacked on four to six occasions. Nearly half

(46%) of the masculine-defined homosexuals claimed they had been assaulted whereas only approximately one-third (31%) of the feminine-defined homosexuals claimed they had been assaulted. No ethnic differences were found for this category.

What this finding indicates is that those inmates who did *not* consider themselves to be feminine were assaulted more often than those homosexuals who did consider themselves to be feminine. One explanation for these differences is the fact that many of the feminine homosexuals felt defenseless when sexually pressured or physically assaulted and quickly "gave in." The masculine homosexuals, on the other hand, were not as quick to succumb to this pressure and thereby experienced greater amounts of physical assault. Furthermore, many of the feminine-defined homosexuals were more prone to have sex when "hit on." As one such inmate stated, "Not only is it easier for us in the long run to have sex when we're pressured . . . [but also] how can you rape the willing?"

The respondents were also asked about the *number of disciplinary writeups* (or 115s) they had received from the prison staff for sexual conduct (or for being caught in a "compromising position"). The majority of the homosexuals (71%) had received disciplinary writeups. There is a certain irony here, of "blaming the victim," since the prison "allows" them to be pressured. Nearly two-thirds (64%) of the men had received from one to three such writeups. The most writeups reported by one inmate was nine.

## Homosexual Experience or Feelings

The major focus of our survey of homosexuals in prison was a twenty-six-item questionnaire which asked about these inmates' feelings and experiences as homosexuals in prison. For each of the twenty-six statements, the respondents were asked if they agreed, disagreed, or were "not sure" of their response. The results of this questionnaire are presented in Appendix Table 19 (see pages 254–255), and their responses are more fully discussed in the three sections to follow.

## SEXUAL IDENTITY

The homosexual sample was asked to respond to a series of statements aimed at gathering information concerning sexual identity. One item, the statement "I am a homosexual," investigated the degree to which they identified as being homosexual. The vast majority (90%) reported that they *strongly* agreed with the statement and the reminder merely agreed with the statement. All of the respondents defined themselves as homosexual.

Close to one-fifth of the homosexuals (19%) also identified themselves as bisexual. Racial differences were noted here, as a higher proportion of whites—over one-third (35%)—identified themselves as also being bisexual compared to the black homosexuals (14%) and the Mexican-American homosexuals (6%).

This homosexual group who also defined themselves as being bisexual differed from the bisexual group reported in Chapter 4. In the bisexual sample in our general prison survey, none identified himself as also being homosexual. In other words, they viewed themselves as being heterosexual and bisexual, not homosexual and bisexual as this group does. In that regard, the bisexual group in the total sample, or the "heterosexual-defined bisexual," was more likely to be black and more likely to report playing only the dominant role in male sex. Their behavior, as we noted, was comparable to the sexual behavior of the heterosexual jocker with the difference being a cognitive one in terms of how they defined and integrated the fact that they were sexually active with other males. The group of homosexuals, on the other hand, or the "homosexual-defined bisexual," was more likely to be Caucasian and more likely to report greater sexual diversity, assuming both active and passive roles.

Racial differences were also noted among the homosexual group in response to the statement concerning whether they identified as *acting more feminine* than masculine. As Appendix Table 20 shows, over four-fifths of the Mexican-American homosexuals (82%) and nearly two-thirds of the black homosexuals (65%) identified themselves as being feminine. Only slightly more than one-quarter of the white homosexuals (27%) identified themselves as being more feminine (see page 256).

In general, the homosexual group appeared to be content with their sexual identity. Three-quarters of the respondents (76%) agreed with the statement that they were happy and satisfied with their sexual identity. Ethnic differences were noted, however. Both the black and white homosexuals were twice as likely as were the Mexican-American homosexuals to report being content. For example, 87% of the black homosexuals and 85% of the white homosexuals agreed with the statement concerning being content with one's sexual identity. Only 41% of the Mexican-American homosexuals agreed with the statement; moreover, one-third (35%) of the Chicanos disagreed with the statement (as opposed to not being sure). Additionally, those homosexuals who were content with their sexual identity reported that prison conditions and treatment seemed *more* favorable for homosexuals.

Four-fifths (84%) of the total homosexual sample disagreed with the statement that they would rather be straight. In fact only one homosexual respondent indicated a preference for being heterosexual, although some (15%) indicated that they were not sure as to how they felt.

Three-quarters (78%) of the group disagreed with the

statement that they would rather be a female. However, some inmates (13%) did indicate such a preference. Interestingly, no racial differences were noted for those preferring to be a female. Whereas black and Chicano homosexuals were more likely than whites to identify as being feminine, blacks and Chicanos were *not* more likely to prefer being a female.

If any general trend could be noted, it was that the homosexual group indicated a preference for being more masculine. Close to two-fifths of the homosexuals either agreed (14%), or were not sure (29%), that they would rather be more masculine.

In summary, the homosexuals sampled in this prison appeared to be generally satisfied with their sexual identity, although this was more true for the black and white homosexuals than it was for the Mexican-American homosexuals.

TREATMENT IN PRISON

Several items allowed the homosexual inmates to voice their opinions concerning how they had been treated in prison.

With regard to *treatment by the staff,* the homosexual group was asked if they felt the staff was sensitive to the problems of homosexual inmates. Close to half of the respondents (48%) did not feel that the staff was sensitive; however, a surprisingly sizable group (35%) *did* feel that the staff was sensitive and that they made an attempt to protect the homosexuals. The remainder of the respondents were undecided. But as we mentioned in an earlier chapter, the homosexuals we interviewed felt that the staff could be much *more* sensitive to the needs of the homosexual inmates. (We deal more fully with these staff and prison personnel issues in the concluding chapter.)

Racial differences were noted on this subject. Black and white homosexuals were twice as likely as Mexican-American homosexuals to feel that the staff was sensitive to their needs. The difference in the responses of the Mexican-American homosexuals needs some clarification. The associate superintendent in charge of inmate services pointed out that the Chicano homosexuals were constantly complaining to the staff. This administrator felt that what differential treatment they might have received was due to their own personal negativism, and that there was no substantive validity to their feeling that they were purposely singled out and mistreated by the prison staff.

Nearly three-fifths of the inmates (59%) agreed that the *staff tended to tolerate homosexual relationships* between inmates. Slight racial differences were recorded: two-thirds of the black homosexuals (68%) versus half of the white and Chicano homosexuals agreed with the statement. In general, the homosexuals in prison felt that the staff tolerated same-sex relationships.

As for *treatment by other inmates,* the homosexuals were asked if they felt that homosexual inmates were looked down upon and treated with disrespect by other inmates. Over three-quarters of the homosexuals (78%) agreed that this was the case. Racial differences were also noted in response to this question. The black homosexuals were more likely to feel that the other inmates treated them with disrespect than were the Caucasian and Mexican-American homosexuals. Over 90% of the black homosexuals felt that the other inmates looked down upon them and disrespected them.

The homosexual group was also asked if they *were currently hooked up.* The vast majority (88%) reported that they were currently involved in such a relationship. And although all three ethnic groups reported high rates of involvement, a larger proportion of Mexican-American homosexuals than of black and white homosexuals reported being currently hooked up.

The homosexuals were asked two questions germaine to our primary issue of sexual exploitation. One question asked if they had *been frequently pressured sexually* by other inmates. The second question asked if they had *often been pressured into having sex* against their will. Whereas the first question sought responses concerning the degree to which they had been pressured (i.e., sexual innuendo, sexual harassment, verbal and physical threats), the second question sought an indication of the frequency with which they were pressured or forced into having sex itself. Although the responses to both these questions were similar, more inmates reported pressure (53%) than reported actually being forced into having sex (41%). Further, some inmates were not sure as to whether or not they had been pressured (5%) or had been actually forced into having sex (10%). Slightly less than half of the homosexuals (49%) reported they had *not* been pressured.

This indicates that close to half of the homosexuals in our sample had been under some form of sexual pressure, and that many had been pressured to the point of forced sexual encounters. Ethnic differences were once again apparent. Two-thirds of the white homosexuals reported that they had frequently been pressured. A lesser percentage of Chicano and black homosexuals reported such pressure. For example, in response to the more critical statement "I have often been pressured into having sex . . ." one-third of the Chicano homosexuals (35%) and one-fourth of the black homosexuals (27%) concurred, compared to two-thirds of the white homosexuals (65%). This significant finding is shown on Appendix Table 21 (see page 256).

As we have discussed throughout this study, the Caucasians in prison (both homosexual and heterosexual) are much more likely to be "hit on" than are the Mexican-Americans and blacks. With two-thirds of the white homosexuals reporting having been forced into sex against their will, incarceration leads to a situation in which whites are disproportionately likely to be victimized.

One item investigated the involvement of this homosexual group in some form of *therapy*. Three-quarters (76%) indicated they had *not* received such therapy while one-quarter (24%) reported that they had.

In terms of how they were interpersonally treated in prison, the homosexuals were critical of their treatment by others and this appears to be an area that warrants improvement. Based on the results of this study, the homosexuals felt that the staff was not as sensitive as they could be to the problems of homosexual inmates although the staff was viewed as generally tolerating homosexual relationships. Concerning staff sensitivity, the Mexican-American homosexuals were the most critical. With respect to treatment by other inmates, the vast majority of the homosexuals felt that they were treated with disrespect and that the other inmates looked down on them.

The vast majority of homosexuals reported being hooked-up, or involved in a relationship. Nearly half of the homosexuals reported having been pressured into having sex with the Caucasians reporting much higher incidences of sexual victimization and exploitation. And, finally, some of the homosexuals indicated they were receiving some form of therapy.

SEXUAL EXPERIENCES IN PRISON

The respondents were asked several questions concerning their *preference* or choice *in sexual partners*. One question, for example, asked them if they preferred heterosexuals ("straight trade") for sexual partners. Racial considerations explained the sharp division within the homosexual group in response to their choice of sexual partners. Both black and Mexican-American homosexuals indicated that they preferred jockers or studs ("trade") as their sexual partners; white homosexuals indicated that they preferred having sex with other homosexuals. This difference in choice of sexual partners further supports our contention that the sharp dichotomy in sexual roles played by prison homosexuals is based on ethnic and cultural considerations. Black and Chicano "queens" are expected to hook up with a "real man." As would be expected, those homosexuals who defined themselves as feminine *also* indicated a preference for the jockers as sexual partners. Two-thirds of the white homosexuals (69%), on the other hand, indicated that they did *not* prefer "straight trade" as a sexual partner.

The homosexuals were asked if they preferred masculine homosexuals for sexual partners. The vast majority (89%) indicated this was also their preference. No ethnic differences were noted here. Conversely, very few (10%) indicated that they preferred feminine homosexuals as their sexual partner. As one effeminate homosexual who was interviewed informed us, "How can you expect me to have sex with my 'sister'?"

The homosexuals were asked if they had often had sex with someone for profit. One-third of the respondents (35%) indicated they had "hustled" while in prison. Once again ethnic differences were noted. The black homosexuals were more likely (46%) to have had sex for profit than either the white homosexuals (31%) or the Mexican-American homosexuals (18%). Quite likely these hustling patterns were a carry-over into prison of behavior that had been occurring on the street (however, since we did not include a question as to "hustling" experience prior to incarceration, this statement is merely a supposition).

The homosexuals were asked two questions concerning their *preferred* (as opposed to actual) *role* when having sex. One question asked them if they preferred performing oral copulation to being anally penetrated. Only one-fourth of the homosexuals indicated they preferred performing fellatio. Moreover, differences by ethnic group in response to this question *were* statistically significant (at the .0004 level). The white homosexuals were more likely to indicate a preference for being active in oral sex whereas the black and Chicano homosexuals were more likely to indicate a preference for being passive in anal sex.

The respondents were also asked if they always took the passive role when having sex. Three-quarters (73%) stated that they always assumed this role. Again, ethnic differences were noted: the white homosexuals were less likely always to take the passive role when having sex. As we have often noted, the white homosexuals were much more diverse in their types of sexual activity. This diversity was also common among bisexual and heterosexual Caucasians.

The respondents were asked if they had *frequently dressed in drag* (worn women's clothing) while on the streets (before incarceration). One-third of the sample group (34%) reported that they had dressed in drag. Nearly half of the black homosexuals (46%) indicated having this experience, and they were twice as likely to have dressed in drag as were Chicano and white homosexuals.

The respondents were asked if they had *more sex in prison* than on the street. Only one-quarter of the homosexuals (24%) reported that they agreed with the statement that they had more sex in prison, although a comparatively high number (18%) indicated that they were not sure. Ethnic differences were again noted. Over one-third of the Chicano homosexuals (35%) and nearly one-fourth of the black homosexuals (24%) reported that they had more sex in prison than on the street. This was particularly true for those homosexuals who defined themselves as feminine.

The respondents were also asked if they had *better sex*

*in prison* than on the street. For most of the homosexuals (77%) this had not been the case—sex was better outside of prison. Yet one-fifth of the black homosexuals (22%) indicated that they had better sex *in* prison. These homosexuals were also more likely to define themselves as feminine.

This finding raises an interesting point. It appears that for some effeminate homosexuals—particularly the black "queens" in prison—sexual activity is viewed as more frequent and more favorable in prison than it is on the streets. In other words, for some of these homosexuals it appears that their role carries some degree of status in prison; outside of prison, however, appearing effeminate does not give them that same degree of status since (extreme) effeminate behavior in men is not highly valued in either the black subculture or in the contemporary gay subculture. Furthermore, because the prison sexual code expects (all) homosexuals to be sissies, those homosexauls who in fact are effeminate are likely to be, at the very least, tolerated within the prison context. On the outside, however, that behavior is not culturally supported or sanctioned. Thus some black homosexuals, and to a lesser degree Mexican-American homosexuals, report having had better sex in prison. By contrast, only one white homosexual reported that sex had been better in prison.

The respondents were asked if most of their *sexual partners* in prison *considered themselves to be heterosexual* (straight). The vast majority (89%) responded affirmatively, and once again this reflects the realities of the prison sexual code which expects a homosexual to have sex with a "man." In terms of ethnic patterns, *all* the Mexican-American homosexuals reported that their sexual partners were men who considered themselves to be straight.

Finally, in what could be considered a question which comprehensively looks at the totality of the homosexual experience in prison, the respondents were asked if most of their sexual *partners respected them as a person.* Only slightly more than one-third of the homosexuals (38%) felt that they were respected. Again, ethnic differences were noted. More black homosexuals (46%) indicated they thought their sexual partners respected them than did white homosexuals (39%) or Mexican-American homosexuals (18%). It should be pointed out, however, that one-fourth of the homosexual group (26%) felt that their partners had not treated them with respect. The responses to this question showed no clear pattern, which indicates that the sexual experience was an individualistic one: some homosexuals had sexual partners who supported them while others had partners who were not as supportive and respectful.

In general with respect to sexual experiences in prison the homosexuals indicated a preference for more masculine men—the blacks and chicanos clearly preferred "straight trade"—and all three ethnic groups preferred more masculine than feminine homosexuals as sexual partners. Ethnic differences explained preferences in type of sexual activity: blacks and Chicanos preferred passivity in anal sex and white homosexuals preferred activity in oral sex. The blacks were more likely to have engaged in sex for profit in prison, and to have dressed in drag outside prison. The more feminine-defined homosexuals indicated they had both more and better sex in prison, leading to our supposition that prison provided this group of effeminate homosexuals with a definite status and role as well as a "captive audience." Most of the homosexuals indicated that their sexual partners were men who considered themselves to be heterosexual. Many of the homosexuals felt that they had not been treated with respect by their sexual partners, although there were some homosexuals in less exploitive relationships who felt that their partners did respect them.

Overriding these patterns, however, was the fact that nearly half of the homosexuals surveyed indicated that they had been sexually pressured into having sex against their will. Furthermore, the vast majority of these homosexual victims of sexual assault were Caucasian; this was true for the vulnerable heterosexual youngsters as well. And, as previously discussed, the homosexual rape victim, like the heterosexual youngster who has been sexually victimized, finds minimal social support or intervention in prison to alleviate his often traumatic experience.

It is interesting to note and compare the social attitudes toward heterosexual rape in society with rape in prison. In recent years the crime of rape has received a great deal of attention from the media and law makers. In California penalties for rape have been increased in severity, now rivaling those for murder. Due largely to the influence of the feminist movement, law enforcement and the court systems have revised their procedures for dealing with rape victims. In many police departments officers are sent to special seminars to learn to deal effectively and compassionately with (female) rape victims, while other departments employ counselors who have been specially trained to handle these cases. Further, there is a major emphasis in society today on providing long-term counseling and social services to rape victims in an attempt to minimize "rape trauma." Rape is now viewed as one of the more abhorrent violent crimes, and rape victims are treated with enlightened compassion and concern.

Sadly, none of this attention or concern has been directed to the issue of prison rape, or to the traumas faced by male rape victims, traumas at least as acute as those experienced by female victims on the streets. In stark contrast, it is extremely rare for a perpetrator of a prison rape to be prosecuted, even when identified, and there are no counseling or support services provided to the victims. It is apparent that society and penal administrators tolerate a double standard in these issues and have refused to acknowledge or effectively deal with the problem.

When questioned about this lack of services, certain prison officials tended to "blame the victim," making such comments as "they asked for it" or "they did nothing to help themselves." This attitude is comparable to the attitude formerly held by police toward the female rape victim.

In summation, as has been clearly shown from the discussion of our data, certain social patterns have developed in prison which in great measure determine how homosexual inmates live their lives. These patterns are based on the convict sexual code and differing ethnic and cultural values imported into the prison setting. Although differences among inmates persist, the general social patterns discussed in the earlier chapters were all substantiated by our study. What we have not yet discussed in detail, however, is the varied "types" of homosexuals that we found in this prison. It is to this discussion that we now turn.

# 8

## Types of Homosexuals in Prison

A comprehensive study published in 1978 by Alan P. Bell and Martin S. Weinberg entitled *Homosexualities: A Study of Diversity Among Men & Women*[17] presented a typology of homosexual identities and lifestyles which is useful, in part, to our study of prison homosexuals. In their study the authors listed five types of homosexuals: the close-coupleds, the open-coupleds, the functionals, the dysfunctionals, and the asexuals.

The *close-coupleds* were those homosexuals who in many ways resemble married heterosexual couples. They prefer sexual monogamy, report fewer sexual problems, and do not regret their sexual orientation. The *open-coupleds* were those men who have one special intimate partner while also maintaining a more open sexual and social relationship. This group, however, was less content, less self-accepting, and less comfortable with their sexual orientation than the close-coupleds.

The *functionals* were those individuals who most closely resemble the heterosexual "swinging singles." The functionals reported wider sexual contacts, they were least likely of all groups to regret being homosexual, and they were actively involved in the gay world. Their adjustment was due in part to their positive self-identites. Yet compared to the close-coupleds, the functionals were more tense and lonely.

The *dysfunctionals* were those individuals who fit the long-held stereotype of the depressed homosexual. The dysfunctionals displayed the poorest self-adjustment, they were the most regretful about their sexual orientation, they had difficulties in sexual functioning, and they were the least successful in meeting other homosexuals for either friendship or sexual involvement.

The *asexuals* were those individuals who had the least amount of involvement with others. They had fewer sexual contacts, and although they reported some sexual problems, they were less interested in sex than the men in the other categories. The asexuals also spent much of their time alone.

This typology provides us with a framework in which to discuss the "homosexualities" of our prison homosexuals. As the data presented in the previous chapter have shown, there is some divergence in the feelings and experiences of homosexuals in prison. This homosexual group is likely as diverse as the homosexual population outside prison although, as we have repeatedly indicated, our prison homosexual population is overrepresentative of men from lower socioeconomic status and ethnic backgrounds, men with effeminate identities, and men who have been strongly affected by the strictures of the prison convict sexual code. As we pointed out in the last chapter, the majority of homosexuals in our study reported generally positive self-identities and positive feelings about their homosexuality. Negative feelings were expressed only in their perceptions of mistreatment and disrespect from the other inmates and the prison staff.

For many homosexuals, it appears that an adjustment to prison life is strongly affected by a concurrent positive adjustment to their roles as homosexuals as defined by the convict sexual code. This prison sexual code, which works to feminize homosexuals, is directly opposed to the goals of the modern gay movement.[18] A positive gay identity attempts to free men from the tyranny of rigid role-playing. It attempts to encourage men to break out of their "prison" (or "closet") existence. It supports their gaining a sense of independence, integrity, and personal well-being—a pride in their identities as homosexuals. Such a "liberation" is not, as we have implied, to be found in the prison environment. In fact quite the opposite occurs. Prison life for homosexuals is influenced by the traditional dictates which work to keep them bound to rigid stereotypic roles—the roles of the submissive, dependent, passive, and weak female—the same roles many women in society have also rejected.

Because the modern gay movement has not developed (or not *yet* developed) in prison, adjustment to homosexual life as it exists behind bars must be measured by criteria different from those used to measure adjustment to gay life for homosexuals outside of prison. In this sense, the definitions for the typologies of homosexualities will need alteration to fit the realities and strictures of prison life.

## Homosexualities in Prison

Summaries of interviews with various homosexuals from our prison sample will be presented and analyzed in this chapter. The excerpts from these case studies were selected for inclusion because their presentations of self in prison reflect the diversity of the types of homosexuals found in the earlier Bell and Weinberg study. We were successful in obtaining interviews with homosexuals who exemplified four of the five categories, although we have had to alter the criteria for inclusion in, and the definitions of, each of the categories. We were unable to conduct interviews with homosexuals who fit the category of asexuals (due to the extreme closeted nature of that type of identity and lifestyle). But we discuss the existence of these individuals as we acknowledged them to be in prison.

## CLOSE-COUPLEDS IN PRISON

The close-coupleds in prison reflect most clearly the male sexual relationships that we presented in Chapter 5. This is, these close-coupleds are comprised of a straight or bisexual jocker and an effeminate homosexual. The close-coupleds in the contemporary gay world, on the other hand, are comprised of two positively affirmed gay men who build a mutually supportive relationship with minimal amount of sex role-playing. The prison close-coupleds develop when the homosexual partner adapts to the submissive sexual role and hooks up with a dominant partner who looks out for the sissy within the context of a "closed" relationship modeled after a traditional marriage in the heterosexual world.

Thus prison close-coupleds are comprised of only those individuals who model their relationship after a heterosexual marriage relationship with the "sissy" playing (and internalizing) the traditional female role in all respects. By contrast, the modern gay close-coupleds are comprised of men who are likely to view each other in comparable ways. This does not mean to imply that sex-role differences are not to be found in modern gay male couples. It just means that gay men are increasingly less likely to construct their relationship along traditional male and female roles with one partner assuming characteristically only one role. If anything, modern gay close-coupleds are likely to explore an androgynous lifestyle, as each member of the relationship asserts both traditional masculine and feminine roles and feelings, and varied sexual behavior. These patterns hold true for those gay men who are comfortable with their sexual orientation and open about their lifestyle.[19]

Although many of the homosexuals in our study were equally comfortable about their lives, the prison convict code expected all homosexuals to act like women. Those homosexuals who conformed to this expectation were able to hook up in relationships which developed the characteristics of the relationships of the close-coupleds in terms of monogamy and stability.

### "Ginger"

"Ginger," for example, has been hooked up with the same man for two years. His relationship with "Bob" is a typical one, with little emotional attachment. Bob keeps the "heat" off him and Ginger provides him with sex whenever Bob wants it, usually from three to four times a week. Outside of sex there is really little involvement. Ginger is expected to wash Bob's clothes for him, a behavior which is typical of most relationships since it fits the so-called woman's role. Ginger does not love Bob, but he states, "We get along good." Ginger, age thirty, is a black effeminate homosexual who has served five years of his life term for second-degree murder. His reported sexual activity is predominantly that of the submissive partner.

### "Silky"

Another inmate, "Silky," fits the profile of the typical homosexual inmate in prison. Like Ginger, Silky is a young (twenty-four) black inmate who has served four years in prison. His relationship with "Big Al," however, is closer than most (or so he claims). Big Al treats him well and Silky has chosen not to have sex with anyone else. They have sex about once or twice a week and Silky is usually passive in anal intercourse. Although Silky reported having been verbally intimidated on twenty occasions (by other inmates prior to his being hooked up), he has never actually been physically or sexually assaulted.

*"Nina"*

Ethnic differences in these close-coupled relationships for the prison homosexuals are noted with "Nina." Nina is a twenty-two-year-old Mexican-American who has served over half his two-year term for burglary. Nina is quiet, soft-spoken, and very passive. Nina told us that he would not turn down any Mexicans who approached him for sex, not because he would necessarily want to have sex with them, but because he feels "it is my place to have sex with them." In this prison Nina is hooked up with a Chicano named "Indio" who is typically dominant and possessive. He makes all the decisions for Nina and takes care of all Nina's financial affairs. Nina in turn, assumes the role of the "faithful wife" and performs such domestic chores as washing his clothes and cleaning up his room. Nina would never ever think of having sex with anyone else unless Indio told him to, which is highly unlikely. Nina's sexual activity has been exclusively passive.

Open-Coupleds in Prison

What differentiates the open-coupleds in prison from the close-coupleds is the greater "openness" to their relationship since both partners are not so sexually exclusive. In terms of the role for the homosexual partner, however, the convict sexual code maintains the expectation of femininity. In all instances the interviews with homosexuals involved in either close-coupled or open-coupled relationships indicated that they were (and enjoyed) adhering to the stereotype of "street sissy." Furthermore, in all but one instance it was the black homosexuals who assumed this role, adopted female names, and referred to themselves (and were referred to by others) in the feminine gender. In all respects they developed a feminine identity, an identity which had been adopted on the streets before incarceration.

## "Kippy"

"Kippy," for example, reflects the typical homosexual found in the open-coupleds in prison. He is a twenty-six-year-old black who has served five years of a life sentence for murder. Since his arrival in this prison he has been hooked up six times. Kippy is well accepted by the other blacks. He is like most of the black queens who, once they have established themselves in prison and become known and accepted, are more or less considered part of the community and are free to do as they wish. Nevertheless, most of them still maintain one particular person to whom they primarily answer, and who is responsible for their welfare. Kippy's current partner is a black man named "Sterling." They have a loose relationship and usually have sex only once or twice a week. Other than that, they do not spend much time together.

Kippy associates mainly with other black queens. He tends to be quite sexually active whenever and wherever he can. Since coming to this prison he has had sexual experiences with seventy different inmates. Nearly all of his sexual activity involved the submissive role and he reported having been anally penetrated approximately 200 times. He has been pressured into sex on only two occasions. Kippy has also received four citations for sexual conduct.

### "Monique"

"Monique," like Kippy, has been quite sexually active in prison. Monique is a forty-year-old black who was brought up in the South and so considers himself to be a "real Southern lady." However, when he gets provoked he can turn vicious and dangerous. Monique has been confined in a federal maximum-security prison and is "joint wise." He can take care of himself, and to insult him in any way is to ask for trouble. In this regard Monique represents another common prison type—the effeminate black homosexual who has hardened to prison life and has developed aggressive and manipulative patterns.

Monique prefers young white boys for sex partners, and is quite sexually aggressive. He is currently hooked up with a twenty-four-year-old white inmate, Carl. Monique is not dependent on Carl, however, nor is he dominated by him. In addition, Monique has been known to pay young heterosexual white boys to have sex with him.

As with most prison queens Monique is "outfront" as a homosexual and refers to everyone as "darling" or "honey." He and his partner have sex about twice a week, although they are seldom seen together in public. Sexually, Monique plays the passive role and reported having been anally penetrated nearly 400 times. He indicated that he had never been pressured into sex nor had he received a citation for sexual conduct.

### "Terry"

Another example of a prison homosexual who is a open-coupled is "Terry." Terry is thirty-two and black, and has served eighteen months of a two-year sentence for possession of heroin. Terry is from southern California where he was a drag queen. In prison he is loosely hooked up with a black con called "B.J." who is forty years old. Their relationship is extremely casual and they have sex only about twice a month. Terry is free to have sex with other partners and is promiscuous. On one occasion he was physically assaulted for telling a convict "I'm more of a man than you'll ever be, and more of a woman than you can handle." This resulted in a fist fight and Terry was able to defend himself. Like the others previously mentioned, Terry assumes primarily the submissive sexual role. He reported having sex with thirty different inmates and has been anally penetrated more than 100 times.

### "Mae"

Our last example of the "black prison sissy" is "Mae." Mae is twenty-six and has served four years of his sentence. Mae is coy and energetic and accepts himself for what he is. He is hooked up with an inmate named "Ted" who is twenty-three. Mae is free to do whatever he wishes as long as he first checks with Ted.

Mae is a typical black prison queen and associates with the other black sissies. On Friday night—movie night— the "girls" get all dressed up and can be seen prominently strutting about at the gymnasium where the movies are shown. Mae, like the others, performs the submissive role. He has been pressured into sex on six occasions, has been physically assaulted twice, and has received one disciplinary citation.

### "Carl"

The only Caucasian in our group of open-coupleds maintained an identity as male but assumed a passive, feminine role sexually. "Carl" is thirty-four and has served two of three years for forgery. Before incarceration he worked as a hair stylist. Since coming to prison he has hooked up with two different black convicts, preferring his men, as he stated, "big, black, and muscled." Both of the relationships have been congenial; he is currently involved with a young black named "Stormy."

When Carl first arrived in prison, before he hooked up, he was having sex with both whites and blacks. The whites attempted to "stick" Carl for having sex with blacks. The blacks backed Carl and kept the whites from hurting him. Once a white homosexual hooks up with a black, he is looked down upon and ostracized by many of the hard-core whites, but these whites usually do not try any physical assault for fear of retaliation from the blacks. Carl is attached to Stormy and they are together most of the time, although Carl is free to have sex with other inmates. Carl prefers the submissive sexual role. He reported having been pressured into sex on three occasions. He has not received any disciplinary citations.

FUNCTIONALS IN PRISON

The functionals in prison were distinguished from the close-coupleds and open-coupleds in that they were able to maintain their independence and autonomy. This they accomplished either by maintaining a male identity and masculine image, or by maintaining a female identity that held some status and demanded respect. The homosexuals we are describing as "functionals" appeared to be less dependent on protection from another (heterosexual) inmate.

*"David"*

One of the functionals, *"David,"* is a twenty-four-year-old white inmate who has served eighteen months of a four-year sentence for sales of dangerous drugs. This is his second prison term. David is atypical of a prison homosexual. He grew up in, and is nicknamed, Texas. David is an outfront gay. What distinguishes him from the more typical prison homosexuals is that David is masculine in appearance and has a dominant (or "butch") personality. He is not hooked up with anyone. David prefers having sex with the younger homosexual convicts who are usually willing participants. Because of his dominant mannerisms and aggressive personality, David is accepted by most of the convicts and is not subjected to the normal pressure directed at more passive homosexuals.

David indicated that he "came out" as a homosexual at sixteen. In prison he has had sex with twenty different inmates, and performs all sexual roles except for being passive in anal penetration. David has never been pressured or assaulted, nor has he received conduct citations.

### "McGee"

"McGee" is an example of another functional. He is a forty-two-year-old black inmate who has served half of his four-year prison term. He is very dominant in bearing and mannerisms, and large in physical stature. McGee is very independent and is able to function in prison as he so desires. He is active in the Metropolitan Community Church services for homosexuals, and is a full-time student in the prison college extension program with hopes of earning a Bachelor of Arts degree upon his release.

Because of his physical and personal dominance, he is liked and respected by almost all inmates within his quad. He also tends to look out for the other homosexuals in his quad, and will back them up if they are being unduly pressured or intimidated. He has adopted the role of "big brother." McGee is not hooked up at present, but he has hooked up with other homosexuals in the past. He is intelligent and has an active, inquiring mind. He is a natural leader. McGee is sexually versatile, preferring both heterosexuals and feminine homosexuals for sexual partners. He has never been pressured or assaulted, nor has he received any 115s.

### "John"

Another inmate who has maintained his independence and fits the characteristics of a functional is "John." John is twenty-three years old, white, and has served most of his six-year term for armed robbery. He stated that he more or less "came out" in prison although he had many gay friends on the outside with whom he was not sexually active. His first sexual encounter occurred in another prison with his cellmate. John woke up one night to find his cellmate masturbating. This excited John and he offered to perform fellatio. From that time on while he was in the other prison he had sex regularly with his cellmate, who would reciprocate by masturbating John.

In this prison John is hooked up with a twenty-five-year-old lifer. John stated that there are mutual feelings of attachment between the two of them. They have sex twice a week. His partner kisses him while performing anal intercourse and will masturbate John, but will reciprocate no further. John as been pressured into sex on two occasions by blacks. This occurred when he first arrived in prison and before he hooked up. He does not come across as being a prison homosexual as he is not effeminate, but neither is he overly masculine in appearance.

### "Sylvia"

Another example of a functional homosexual is "Sylvia" who, even though he maintains a feminine identity, is able to achieve his autonomy and independence because of the role he performs in prison.

Sylvia is a thirty-eight-year-old Mexican-American who has been in prison for seven years (this is his second term in prison). He is from the barrio of Riverside, California, and is energetic and self-sufficient. Although he is not hooked up, a couple of Chicano convicts look out for him. Sylvia is quite promiscuous within this Chicano clique and reported having sex with 150 persons. Almost all of his sexual activity involved being passive in anal penetration. Sylvia is able to be so independent because of the "maternal" role that he assumes with the Chicano convicts, and they appear to respect and accept him for it. He has never been pressured into sex nor has he received a disciplinary writeup.

Those homosexuals who assumed the role of functionals in prison differed from the effeminate homosexuals of the close-coupleds or open-coupleds in significant ways. Either their physical size and masculine demeanor demanded respect (as in the cases of David and McGee), or their survival strategy in prison and personality traits allowed them certain flexibility (as in the cases of John and Sylvia). In this regard, the ability to maintain control of their situation and to maintain autonomy if they so desire are the distinguishing characteristics of the functionals. This group was able to be as sexually active as they wished.

## DYSFUNCTIONALS IN PRISON

Certain homosexuals in prison had difficulty in accepting either their own homosexuality or the roles that were forced upon them as homosexuals by the convict prison code. Still others had difficulty fitting into the prison environment because of their mistreatment and rejection by the other inmates; in some instances this was due to the nature of the crimes they had committed (i.e., child molestation) or to unpleasant personality characteristics (i.e., problems in personal hygiene and cleanliness), or to circumstances beyond their control such as physical attractiveness. Because these men were unable to function in a positive way in the prison environment, they were categorized as "dysfunctionals."

### "Russ"

One such dysfunctional was "Russ." Russ is an older white inmate who was sent to prison for child molestation. This is his second offense and he is classified as a mentally disoriented sex offender. Russ is the only homosexual in our entire sample of eighty men who was incarcerated on sexual misconduct charges. (Most such offenders are sent to a state hospital rather than to state prison. A change in policy, however, is currently before the state legislature which would send these men directly to prison.)

Russ is intelligent and articulate. He pays young heterosexual convicts and "kids" for sex, generally performing oral copulation on them. Russ claimed that his relationships with the prepubescent boys outside prison was not forced or violent. His demeanor in prison is soft-spoken and gentle.

Russ was physically assaulted while in the Guidance Center because of his "beef" (criminal charge). Inmates hold child molesters in great contempt. This prison is one of two in the state where child molesters, when they are sent to prison from the mental hospitals, are not segregated from the general prison population.

Russ stated that he had his first male sexual experience

at eight and came out as a homosexual at eighteen. Since coming to this prison he has had sex with twenty different inmates. He assumes both active and passive roles and has never received a citation for sexual conduct. Russ has never been hooked up in prison and has been in therapy. (We were not able to ascertain how successful this therapy has been.) He prefers straight trade for sexual partners and must often pay to have sex.

### "Steve"/"Stephanie"

Another of the dysfunctionals is a twenty-four-year-old white inmate named "Steve" or "Stephanie." This is his first term, for sales of dangerous drugs. Steve is somewhat unsure of his sexual identity, and he does not fully accept his homosexuality. Prior to his arrest he had a steady girlfriend and was having sex with her on a regular basis. He was also frequenting gay bars and having sex with males. In county jail he was forced, under threat of violence, to submit to anal penetration by another inmate. He also voluntarily performed oral sex with his cellmate.

In this prison Steve is hooked up with a dominating white jocker named "Riley," who is also twenty-four. Riley forces Steve to adopt aspects of a feminine role such as shaving his legs. Riley also calls him "Stephanie." Steve tolerates this situation because he does not feel that he has any choice in the matter. In this respect Steve's situation is similar to that of the punks discussed in Chapter 6. Although he does not like being forced to assume the feminine role and he does not feel comfortable in his relationship with Riley, unlike the punks Steve does admit to enjoying sex with males. Steve would prefer having his independence to find his own role. He does not consider himself to be a "broad," although this role is being forced upon him. He did report having sex on a few occasions under furtive conditions with another homosexual on his tier.

Steve is a prime example of the pressure and exploitation to which the homosexuals who will not conform to the feminine stereotype are subjected while in prison. Riley is building his own masculine image at the expense of Steve, and this pressure is causing Steve's confusion (and dysfunction) in prison. Steve also reported that he had been pressured into sex on four occasions and had been physically assaulted once. He has never received a disciplinary writeup.

### "LeRay"

Another type of dysfunctional in prison is "LeRay." LeRay is a young black who is serving a short term for assault. LeRay suffers from what might be defined as a personality disorder. He projects an image of being flighty, naïve, and overly effeminate. Since coming to prison he claimed to have been hooked up with three different inmates. LeRay is too eager and aggressive, which often proves offensive to most of the inmates. He has bleached auburn hair and is very unattractive by any standards. Most of the black convicts joke about him and would never admit to having sex with him. Because of his demeanor and treatment by others, LeRay's behavior is dysfunctional.

In this sense, those homosexuals who can be typed as dysfunctionals appear to be those whose own criminal offenses (in the case of Russ), prison situations (in the case of Steve/Stephanie), or personality characteristics (as in the case of LeRay) have fostered a certain degree of ostracism by the other inmates. This negative treatment, along with their own interpersonal problems, has created a social pattern which best can be designated as "dysfunctional."

## ASEXUALS IN PRISON

None of the thirty homosexuals interviewed reflects behavior which might place him in the category of "asexual." All of these men reported being sexually active. Furthermore, all of the eighty inmates in our sample of homosexuals in prison also admitted to having had sexual encounters. No person we interviewed or sampled who claimed to be homosexual reported not having engaged in sex since coming to prison.

Based on our observations, however, we are sure that there are homosexuals in prison who could be typed as asexuals. It is our belief that some homosexual men in prison fit the qualifications of the asexual in the nonprison population as presented in the Bell and Weinberg study, a group of homosexual men who are "asexual" during their incarceration but who are sexually active as gay men outside the prison environment.

The majority of homosexual men who remain asexual in prison quite likely are those who most reject the prison sexual code which exploits and feminizes the homosexual, and who, because of masculine appearance and dominance, are able to remain "undercover" (or "incognito") or even totally "in the closet" in prison because they do not wish to identify with, or be identified by, the roles that homosexuals are forced to assume. By keeping their homosexual identity hidden, and by presenting an image of being heterosexual, these men are not subjected to the typical pressures. Many of these prison asexuals undoubtedly lead quite active sexual lives as homosexuals outside the prison setting; in this sense these "asexuals" do not fit the category of asexuals that the Bell and Weinberg study found. These men are merely *situationally* asexual. Although we were unable to interview any men who fit this category we estimate them to comprise close to 1% of the total homosexual group.

## IMPLICATIONS OF THE FINDINGS

These five typologies, or types of homosexual identities and experiences as introduced by the earlier study, have obviously been modified to fit the reality of the prison scene. Our "close-coupleds" were those homosexuals who identified strongly as females and who played the traditional feminine role in a relationship with a straight male. Our "open-coupleds" were similar to the close-coupleds although the homosexual member of the pair had greater independence and freedom to engage in sex outside the primary relationship. Our "functionals" were able to maintain more of a personal identity as a gay person. They were able to project their own sense of autonomy, and the pressures to conform to rigid feminine roles were not as common. Our "dysfunctionals" were those homosexuals who had difficulties in dealing interpersonally in the prison environment, for a variety of reasons. Our "asexuals" were those homosexuals who remained closeted and were able to pass as heterosexual.

By contrast, in the gay community that exists outside the prison environment, the common pattern for both close-coupleds and open-coupleds (according to the Bell and Weinberg study) was for the relationships to be comprised of two men who are involved in a mutually supportive way that tends *not* to be modeled along dichotomous male and female lines. In fact, it is quite often those individuals who exhibit exaggerated female roles who are likely to be viewed as dysfunctionals by the modern gay liberationist. There is a decidedly middle-class bias to this view, however, since some working- and lower-class homosexual couples adhere to traditional dichotomous sex roles in their relationships, one partner assuming the masculine ("butch") role and the other assuming the feminine ("femme") role. But even in these lower socioeconomic strata and among ethnic groups socialized in these traditional manners, changes are taking place reflecting the impact of the larger gay movement.

Thus there exists a striking incompatibility between the roles for homosexuals in prison and for homosexuals in the modern gay movement outside of prison. What is viewed as acceptable and expected behavior for homosexuals in prison (e.g., femininity and passive sexual role-playing) is often now viewed as unacceptable behavior for gay men outside prison. Likewise, what is viewed as inappropriate and unacceptable behavior for homosexuals in prison (e.g., the projection for a strong masculine identity similar to that of some of the homosexuals we typed as functionals) is viewed as the new norm or standard for male homosexuals outside prison. This does not mean to imply that all homosexuals are rejecting the model of a relationship which adheres to some distinctions in roles between the two individuals; it just means that the extreme dichotomization in roles is declining as a prototype (and stereotype) of modern gay couples and individuals.

It is this incompatibility which leads us to claim that prison homosexuality is condoned so long as the homosexual assumes the passive feminine role and hooks up with a straight male. Supportive homosexual relationships between two gay men are not condoned or even tolerated in prison. On the other hand it is exactly this type of relationship—a bond between two self-affirming and masculine-defined gay men—that is emerging as the "ideal" in modern gay relationships. In this sense, proponents of this new ideal have difficulty in supporting the effeminate homosexuals (and transvestites and transsexuals) who are present in the gay community (and normative in the prison). To the gay liberationist, a projection of a feminine identity is to embrace one's oppression and to give in to one's oppressor (straight society). This issue and point of view remain devisive for the gay movement.

In the prison environment life for a positively affirmed gay man is quite difficult unless he is willing to play the feminine role and act like a female, or unless he is strong and powerful enough—both physically and mentally—to stand his ground. Gay men are not allowed to develop a relationship, and if one by chance, in the face of almost insurmountable odds, occurs, it could exist only if it remained covert and invisible to the rest of the prison population. "Gay liberation" has not yet entered prison walls in the sense that two gay men can hook up and be together in a visible way.

Although the treatment of homosexuals has generally improved, as our study has shown, there still remain areas of concern. In our judgment, it is the self-affirming homosexuals who have the most difficulty in prison (along with the vulnerable heterosexual "kids"). No matter how self-affirming a person may be, it is most difficult to stand alone in the absence of all social support. The pressure to conform to the convict sexual code which exploits and feminizes homosexuals and punks "breaks" the vast majority of them. This pressure literally "imprisons" them. For those few inmates who are able (or strong enough) to resist, the experience strengthens their inner resolve. However, the rewards offered to the homosexuals for conformity to the prison sexual code, such as "all the dick you want, as often as you want it," are powerful incentives for them to "fall into line."

The thoughts of one better educated and positively affirmed functional homosexual who is caught up in this dilemma of whether or not to capitulate and conform to the code are helpful in understanding the ambivalence some homosexual inmates have toward their prison predicament:

Personally, I have developed over the years a high self-esteem and I place a high value on personal freedom, self-awareness, and growth. I am very secure in my manhood, and have consciously tried to reach a balance between my masculine and feminine tendencies. I am an individualist, and I rebel at the thought of conforming to anybody's, or society's expectations. These characteristics which I have developed and value are definitely not functional within this prison environment. As a result, I find myself somewhat alienated, ignored, and discounted. Were I a dumb brute with bulging muscles, filthy levis, bizarre tattoos, and an overtly hostile attitude, I would be well respected and liked—one of the "homeboys." It's all a matter of values. The attention I do get, I consider demeaning. I can empathize with the complaint of feminists, that they are tired of being regarded as "sex objects."

It's funny. On the streets there were occasions when I used to fantasize what it would be like to be in a position where you were sexually desirable to everyone you came into contact with—where I could virtually have my pick, anytime, anywhere. My existence here is laced with sweet talk, flirting smiles, and sly winks. The other day while walking in the yard, a young black heterosexual inmate called out to me, "Hey, cupcake, what's happening?" This is supposed to turn me on? Or how about this line: "The man in me needs the woman in you."

In one sense I do get a rush off of the attention. At first I was like a kid in a toy shop, and even now I find myself teasing and encouraging in subtle and covert ways. At times I'll encounter a particular inmate who catches my eye, and I'll watch for the opportunity to catch him in the shower, and then I very nonchalantly climb in. Will he get a hard-on? What does it look like? Is it big? The two of us left alone. I'm washing my hair, now facing the other direction, giving him an ass shot, not too obvious, now bending over, rinsing my hair, catching a glimpse—is it getting hard? Yeh, it's growing. Nothing is said, no talk, no acknowledgment. I let him see me checking it out. There, it's standing up straight. My heart's pounding, I've got butterflies. My dick's hard too, I can't help it. He speaks, "See what you do to me?" I, not really wanting to get involved, smile and reply, "What can I say?" I withdraw. I've accomplished my goal; my curiosity is satisfied. I don't want it to go any further. For ten minutes the mouse has become the cat!

Why do I play the game? I don't know, but there is a payoff, a rush, a symbolic conquest. It's only a shallow, physical act, nothing real or meaningful; it's just manipulation of sexual energy. It is a subtle dance. But it sure beats playing chess!

Within me, however, the purist, the would-be sage, takes a dim view of such "lower nature" pursuits. Where is the meaning, the love, the genuine sharing of each other? Am I a moth, driven by the flame of desire? Is there any real meaning or satisfaction in life to be found in erotic games of sensual desire? The same attention that gives me a rush, I also consider demeaning. I am a creative, intelligent person, not just a sex object! No strokes in prison for my intellect, or sensitivity, or personhood. No strokes for what or who I am within. It's all physical desire. They want to use me for my body, to get their rocks off. They want to use my hole to masturbate with. And I still get caught up in the game. At least I know it is a game.

# III

## REACTIONS TO SEX IN PRISON

# 9

# Inmate Attitudes toward Homosexuality

Within the past decade there have been several studies conducted on *homophobia* (originally termed "homoerotic phobia") or the irrational fear or intolerance of homosexuality.[20] One study reported that the best predictor of homophobia in men was a firm belief in the traditional family ideology with father as head of the household and mother submissive to his authority. A belief in a conservative religious philosophy was also indicative of the person who held negative attitudes toward homosexuality.[21] Other studies have concurred that those individuals who were the most negative in their attitudes concerning homosexuality were likely to be from rural backgrounds, to be Caucasian, and to be male.[22] These studies, however, differed on reporting whether chronological age and level of education were significant indicators. Where differences have been noted, the homophobic person is reported to have been generally older and less educated.

We decided to study the attitudes of two subgroups of our prison population to see if their views on homosexuality supported the results of these earlier studies which

had found differences in measures of homophobia. We
were particularly interested in the attitudes of the older
men in this prison group, and in the attitudes of those
inmates who held traditional religious beliefs and maintained an active Christian or Muslim identity in prison.
Our sampling procedures did not replicate these earlier
studies in measuring homophobia, but our interviews and
case studies do provide some insight into the attitudes of
these two groups toward homosexuality in prison.

## OLDER MEN IN PRISON

A recent study on the effects of aging in prison noted
that major differences existed between this population and
the nonprison aging population widely studied and
reported in the gerontological literature.[23] By focusing on
the prisoners' attitudes and behavior toward family, work,
retirement, religion, and politics—as well as their interaction patterns and their perceptions of aging in prison—the
study reported that patterns associated with "normal
aging" do not occur in prison to the same degree. Most
respondents, for example, felt younger than they per-
ceived older people (of similar income and chronological
age) on the outside to feel since prison life insulated them
from the "hard life on the street" and since in prison they
had access to better food, rest, and medical attention.

Data for our sample of older men were gathered
through an open-ended interview schedule using the
methodologies described in the earlier sections of this
book. Of the sixteen men randomly solicited to be interviewed, only twelve complied. The participation rate for
these older men was considerably lower than for other sections of our study. Older men in prison were more suspi-
cious and hesitant about participating in our study.

According to 1977 federal prison figures, prisoners over the age of fifty comprise only 5% of the total national prison population.[24] And according to 1979 statistics of the felon population in the California state prisons, only 3.7% of the prisoners are age fifty or over.[25] In the prison we studied, 118 men are in this age bracket, accounting for 4.7% of the total. The findings reported in this section are based on case studies and interviews of twelve men (or 10% of the total group) between the ages of fifty and sixty-four, as well as participant-observations of prison life and the status and role of the older prisoners.

## THE PRISON CODE AND THE OLDER PRISONER

For the older men, ethnicity and, to a lesser degree, chronological age clearly defined their primary group affiliations. Both the older blacks and Chicanos found greater compatibility and identity among men of similar cultural background, whereas the older whites were more likely to have a more diverse group of contacts. As to interaction with other inmates of different chronological ages, the Mexican-Americans reported contacts with a greater age range than did the Caucasians or blacks, as the following excerpts from the interviews point out.

### "Filmore"

"Filmore" is a sixty-year-old black inmate who has been in prison since the mid-1970s for grand theft. He is practically illiterate and spends most of his time playing dominoes with his black partners around his own age, walking the yard, or watching television. Filmore states that he does not have any trouble getting along with anybody, although his best friends are both black and over sixty.

## *"Wilson"*

"Wilson," sixty-three, is another black inmate who has been incarcerated since 1978 for grand theft. He had been involved with a counterfeiting ring. Wilson's philosophy is "Nobody bothers me, and I don't bother no one else." He associates mainly with blacks and has a "road dog" (friend) who is fifty-four.

## *"Francisco"*

"Francisco," fifty-one, is a Mexican-American and has been in prison since 1977 for sales of stolen property. He associates primarily with a southern California Chicano clique and is seen in the yard with other Chicanos of all ages. He states that he knows that he will be in and out of prison for the rest of his life and that he will never "quit using" (taking heroin). Francisco is recognized as a group leader since "age demands respect" within the Chicano subculture. For the Mexican-American there is considerable mixing of ages within prison. Francisco associates almost exclusively with other Chicanos and has little use for whites or blacks. He is not hostile toward them; he just keeps his distance. Quite often the older men in prison maintain these ethnic boundaries.

## *"Roy"*

"Roy," age fifty-four, is a white inmate who has been incarcerated since 1978 for vehicular manslaughter, a result of drunk driving. He admits to being an alcoholic and is active in Alcoholics Anonymous. He stated that he associates mainly with other white inmates although he tries to be friendly with most everyone. He does have one close white friend who is forty-six.

Of the remaining eight men who were interviewed, all but two indicated having close friends in prison. As we have observed, the primary associations for both whites and blacks are other inmates of similar age. However, there is a degree of casual mixing with younger men—for instance, when playing cards or when working on the job. Among Chicanos, however, age barriers are much less pronounced and the older men are often revered by the younger Chicanos and hold positions of respect and authority within the cliques. Further, the language factor tends to solidify and insulate the Chicanos. In this regard the Chicanos appear to be more ethnically exclusive and less age conscious in their interaction patterns.

## PARTICIPATION IN PRISON SEX

Only three of the twelve older men interviewed had had sexual encounters while in prison. Francisco reported having had sexual experiences with "punks" on twenty occasions this term, and had been hooked up with punks in prior terms. He takes great pride in his sexual prowess and in being "muy macho." He is also a married heterosexual on the outside.

### "Theodore"

"Theodore," age fifty, is a black inmate who is divorced. He reported having had four sexual encounters in his five years of incarceration. In each instance he had been orally copulated by a "sissy" on his tier. He initiated the sexual encounters.

### "Charles"

"Charles," fifty, and white, was the only "open" homosexual in this sample of older men. Other "closeted" homosexuals refused to participate in the study. Older homosexuals, shaped by the societal realities of a more hostile period, appear to be much less open and self-accepting than the younger homosexuals in prison.

Charles has been incarcerated for ten years for first-degree murder. He killed his next-door neighbor to retaliate for a previous altercation. Charles had his first homosexual experience while in prison and is now attracted to younger men, straight or gay. He is not effeminate, which distinguishes him from many of the younger homosexuals. He will pay for sex if necessary, although he prefers to establish an ongoing exclusive relationship with one person in exchange for his protection and favors. Charles gets along well with almost everyone. Although he does not advertise his sexual proclivities, neither does he hide them. Most of the convicts and staff are aware of his sexual activities and accept them as part of prison life.

Since Charles "came out" while in prison, he has had no prior contact with the outside gay subculture or movement. He does subscribe, however, to some gay periodicals and magazines, and he is well read and aware. Because of the amount of time he has spent in this prison, and his large stature, he is totally self-sufficient, and he demands a degree of respect from both the staff and other inmates.

## "Convicts" versus "Inmates"

As other researchers have noted,[26] distinctions can be drawn between "convicts" and "inmates" in terms of the prisoner's adaptation to the prison code. To many prisoners, a "convict" is a man who identifies with the prison roles and subculture and who conducts himself accordingly. The convict is a hard-core prisoner, as opposed to an "inmate" who is a person doing time but who does not consider himself to be a "convict" and does not conform to the prison cultural expectations. These distinctions are drawn by both groups, and the "inmates" are generally looked upon with contempt by the "convicts," although this is more true among the younger men.

Whether or not a man in prison is socialized into becoming a "convict" is a matter of his own personal self-esteem and values. As can be seen by their statements, most of the older men in our study do not consider themselves "convicts." For the most part they were first-termers who merely wanted to leave the prison as soon as possible.

Only three of the older prisoners interviewed considered themselves to be "convicts." They shared the total antiestablishment and antisocial outlook of the other "cons" and were totally committed to the prison code and values. But, like everything else, these older cons tended to be more complacent than the younger ones. However, these "convicts" were more likely to engage in sex because it is part of the prison sexual scripts with which they identify.

### "Ross"

The comments of one older prisoner who considered himself an "inmate" best reflect this contrast. "Ross," age fifty-nine, is a white inmate in prison since 1978 for embezzlement. He is a first-termer and is married. He is quiet and intelligent and was involved in a securities fraud scheme. He has a grown son who is an architect and gets regular conjugal visits with his wife. Prior to his arrest he was an investment counselor. Ross is a good jail-house lawyer and earns money doing legal work for other inmates.

Ross has not had any prison sexual experiences, but he is not against homosexuals or homosexuality in prison for those who wish to participate. His only real friend is another white inmate who is around forty. Ross says that he has not had trouble "getting along," that he stays out of the television room, and that he does not get involved in any of the "convict games." He neither identifies with, nor participates in, the convict code, and states that the best way to survive in prison is "to mind your own business and to do as you are told."

## COPING STRATEGIES AND LIFE SATISFACTION

It appears that these older "inmates" in this medium-security prison have developed coping strategies which allow them to exist with minimal stress. Although they appear to be resigned to the fact that they are serving time, "life on the tier" seems to provide them with sufficient social support. In comparison to younger prisoners, the older men seem to be somewhat more stable and mature and less prone to get involved in fights, drugs, sex, and other activities which may result in conflicts and trouble. One respondent, for example, stated that the reason the older men do not get into as much trouble is that they are too old to compete and they know it. If he were younger, he said, he would be out "raising hell' with the rest of them, but continued that the physical realities of age force older inmates to "mellow out and keep a low profile."

Likewise the older men tend to be more stable in their jobs and to work in more substantial jobs than the younger prisoners. Ten of the twelve men interviewed held jobs in prison. Most of them have trades which they brought in with them from the streets. Also, over the years they have developed work habits and are better skilled, and hold better attitudes toward maintaining a steady job. Thus the staff trusts older men and prefers them for those jobs that demand a degree of responsibility, such as in the industries, plant maintenance, and upper-level clerk jobs. There are ethnic considerations involved here, however. Many of the older blacks and Mexicans are less educated than the whites and do not have the job skills that the whites do. Yet while their skills may not equip them for the same caliber of job, they still tend to be more stable workers than the younger convicts.

Most of the older men interviewed cooperate with the prison staff and keep a low profile, and they have little trouble getting along with the other inmates. Furthermore, the older men in our study had maintained close contact with spouses and other family members. One man gets frequent visits with his wife and his two grown children; another gets occasional visits with his five children. In fact, nine of the twelve men interviewed maintained ongoing relationships with family members. This helps the inmate in that the family remains a major source of primary relationships.

PRISON POLICY AND PLACEMENT PRACTICES

Another factor in shaping the atmosphere for all older prisoners in this setting is the prison placement policy. Although distinctions between older and younger prisoners remain true for each prison, the prison situation itself may vary by institution. For example, according to our informants one institution in the state of California is comprised of younger men and is considered to be the most violent of all the institutions in the state, while the real "oldtime convicts" are housed in another maximum-security prison where there is relatively little overt violence. The older cons are less likely to continue to have a need to prove their "manhood" or establish a name for themselves. The prison games are the young man's games.

While in county jail and in some of the hard-core joints the younger men may try to exploit or pressure the older men, disrespect them, or even ignore them. In the medium-security prison we studied, however, the older men are generally treated with respect.They are included in both work and leisure activities, and they are left alone if they wish to do their own time.

As with the case of the homosexuals, the staff tends— through their classification procedures—to place the non-hard-core older men in institutions such as this where the atmosphere is less tense. Also, some of the older cons who have proved themselves to be cooperative and non-troublemakers are transferred here from other prisons.

## Discussion of the Findings

Men over the age of fifty in this medium-security prison appear to be able to cope satisfactorily with their situation. For these men, life in prison is what they make of it since—unlike the younger men—they are not pressured into roles they may try to fight against. Trouble in prison mainly comes to those who ask for it or to those, in the case of the homosexuals and vulnerable youngsters, who can be successfully exploited. Older men, both gay and straight, tend to have an easier time because of their more mature approach to life in general, because of their socialization to more traditional values such as work, and because they are simply not as attractive as younger men. The effect of the convict subculture and sexual code appears to influence the behavior of the older inmate to a lesser degree than it does the younger inmate, although ethnic differences and the inmate's self-identity as a "convict" are mitigating factors.

In this prison men over the age of fifty are uncommon and homosexual men over fifty are rarer still. Most of the older men are not sexually active. The prison sexual scene is more or less a young man's activity. Although these older men tend not to engage in prison sex, they do not appear to be any more or less homophobic than the younger men. Their attitude toward homosexuality and homosexuals is, as in most other things, "live and let live."

## INTERVIEWS WITH INMATE RELIGIOUS LEADERS

In the prison system studied, an estimated 6% of the men regarded themselves as Christians (or Born-Again Christians). Approximately 150 men spent most of their free time in the chapel area and were active members in the prison Christian community. Many of these inmates came from Christian families but had in their own words, "gone astray." In prison they reverted back to the Christian beliefs that they had held as children. Often these men would rationalize their crime by stating that everyone sins and, since God forgives them their sins, by taking Christ into their lives they feel they have repented. To repent, in prison jargon, means that one has "turned around" (turned away from crime) or that one has "gone the other way." By stating this the inmate is informing the other convicts that he has made a commitment to lead a Christian life.

This pattern holds true for both homosexual and heterosexual inmates. Once a homosexual embraces a Christian identity, he is socialized into that identity and expected to give up his homosexual activity. The Christian heterosexual is also expected not to engage in prison sex.

In this prison there were several homosexuals who interacted with the Christian clique. From our observations and from informal discussions with them, none appeared to have given up his homosexual identity, although they reported fewer incidents of sexual activity than the non-Christian homosexuals. One reason given by many of these homosexuals for maintaining a "Christian identity" was that this served as protection from harassment by the other prisoners. Those men involved with the Christian group are by and large left alone since these men, if hit on, are more likely to pass this information on to their ministers who in turn report these occurrences to the prison officials. The convicts realize that there is a channel between the Christians and the prison authorities and so generally leave the Christians alone. Therefore those homosexuals who identified with the Christian clique not only had a support group, but they also had an opportunity to escape from being exploited.

To obtain the religious attitudes toward homosexuality in prison, the inmate leaders of the prison religious community were approached to be interviewed. The four interviews conducted were with the three prominent white leaders of the Christian faiths and one black leader of the Muslim faith. As the interviews will show, with respect to issues concerning homosexuality the black Muslim held slightly more liberal and less dogmatic views than did the Christian leaders. The interviews show that those men who hold traditional religious views appear to be more homophobic than those men who reflect the attitudes and practices of the general prison population, thus supporting our hypothesis stated at the beginning of this chapter. As the earlier studies on homophobia documented, holding strict religious beliefs and supporting homosexual activity are virtually incompatible behavioral patterns.

INTERVIEW WITH CHRISTIAN INMATE #1

Q: Do you feel that a homosexual act between consenting adults is
    wrong?
A: It's wrong for the person who knows to do right. From God's stand-
    point, homosexuality is wrong.
Q: What do you think causes people to become homosexuals?
A: Speaking from a spiritual point of view, I'd say that there was a time

in their life when they opened the door to demon activity. This demon is a spiritual being without a physical body but has a mind, will, and emotion. No person is a homosexual because God didn't create any homosexuals. He created man and woman. What the demon does is seek entrance into a human body through a door that is opened by the person. Once in, it seeks to control the mind, will, and emotion of the person.

Q: Do you feel that homosexuals should be granted full legal and social rights?

A: God loves the person. He just doesn't like what the person is doing. So I would say that he should still be treated in love by the society because he is under attack by this demon and needs help. He should be treated as a human being and not as a homosexual because he is being influenced by a foreign being and doesn't know it.

Q: Do you feel homosexual acts between consenting adults should be illegal?

A: I don't think there should be a law against sexual acts. If there is no law against a man having sex with a woman out of wedlock, then there shouldn't be a law against any other type of sex, as long as it is between consenting adults. The law of God is written on every man's heart concerning what is morally right and wrong. I believe every man should be fully persuaded in his own heart what is right and wrong concerning sex, and not by written law.

Q: Do you think that homosexual inmates have a harder time in prison than heterosexual inmates due to pressure and discrimination?

A: Some do and some don't.

Q: Do you feel that the prison should do more or less in the way of protecting homosexual inmates?

A: Should do more for the sake of those who are being pressured against their will.

Q: Do you agree that the Metropolitan Community Church should conduct services for homosexuals here in prison?

A: Sure, I went to one of their meetings and I think so. They get to learn that God loves them in spite of their sexual condition.

Q: Do you believe that masturbation is wrong?

A: In the sight of God masturbation is an abomination because it is a waste of the seed. But it goes back to every man must be persuaded in his own heart what is right for him.

Q: Do you believe that premarital intercourse between a man and woman is wrong, if they love each other?

A: In the Christian community it is wrong for them to have sex before being legally married. However, that law is only for the Christians (Born Again) and not for the non-Christian.

*Q:* Do you think that sexual activity between inmates is very common here in prison?

*A:* Sure.

*Q:* Do you think that forced or pressured encounters are very common here in prison?

*A:* Every once in a while I hear of one.

*Q:* In society in general, do you feel that the authorities should attempt to legislate morality, or do you feel that this should be left up to the discretion of the individuals involved?

*A:* I'm not sure about that question. I would be inclined to say that it should be left up to the individual.

*Q:* What is your opinion of the "Moral Majority" movement among fundamentalists? Do you believe that the church should take an active role in influencing politics and political candidates? Do you believe that Christians should seek to force their views and values on others in society?

*A:* From my understanding of the Word of God, in the Old Testament man was under the law. The New Testament is a new covenant for a newly created people and there is a new law governing the people under this covenant, and the emphasis is on God's Grace and not the law. Non-Christians are unable to keep God's laws; therefore we believers would be wasting our time trying to force it on them. God does not force Himself on any man, so we who are partakers of God's nature should follow His principles and not try to force our beliefs and convictions on those who don't want to hear it.

*Q:* Is there any other statement or remarks that you would like to add to this study?

*A:* I believe that we [Christians] who are in the know, and see things as God sees them, ought to allow God to reach out through us in love and meet the needs of those who are under attack by the rulers of darkness of this world.

## INTERVIEW WITH CHRISTIAN INMATE #2

*Q:* Do you feel that a homosexual act between consenting adults is wrong?

*A:* Yes, primarily because I subscribe to the written Word, the Bible, and it is clearly outlined in the Bible that it is wrong.

Q: What do you think causes people to become homosexuals?

A: No one particular cause, a variety of factors—some being heredi-tary—but most being environmental. That is my own personal experience from talking with homosexuals.

Q: Do you feel that homosexuals should be granted full legal and social rights?

A: I tend to be conservative in my personal views. I realize that society is moving in a more tolerant direction due primarily to the vocal-ness of the homosexual minority. The problem is that it doesn't stop with their just being accepted. They tend to use their positions to foster their cause and to disseminate their lifestyle.

Q: Do you feel that homosexual acts between consenting adults should be illegal?

A: Boy, that's a rough one. I don't believe that you can legislate morality. What standards pertain to me as a Christian do not necessarily per-tain to non-Christians. Nevertheless, personally speaking (not as a representative of the Christian community) I suspect that to stop legislating morality would be a relaxation leading to more compro-mise. However, I don't see the law as the best way to accomplish that end.

Q: Do you think that homosexual inmates have a harder time in prison than heterosexual inmates due to pressure and discrimination?

A: Not as much in this institution, but in most prisons yes, definitely.

Q: Do you feel that this prison should do more or less in the way of protecting homosexual inmates?

A: Not encourage, but protect. If they are experiencing physical prob-lems by all means they should protect them.

Q: Do you agree that the MCC should be allowed to come and conduct services for homosexuals here in prison?

A: No, I'm opposed to the MCC personally. [Interviewer asked why.] Because of my adherence to the Word of God. Homosexuality is dia-metrically opposed to the Word of God. I can't conceive how any-one could attempt to support it in the name of religion. It's too basic a contradiction.

Q: Do you believe that masturbation is wrong?

A: For me, it's wrong. I think it's between the individual and God. The Word of God is pretty clear on it, however.

Q: Do you believe that premarital intercourse between a man and a woman is wrong, if they love each other?

A: Yes.

*Q:* Do you think that sexual activity between inmates is very common here in prison?

*A:* What do you mean by common? I feel maybe 30% of the population probably engages in homosexual activity on an ongoing basis. There are probably many more who have had isolated experiences.

*Q:* Do you think that forced or pressured encounters are very common here in prison?

*A:* Probably initially a high percentage of homosexual activity on the part of younger inmates coming into the institution is pressured, and then it becomes a way of coping.

*Q:* In society in general, do you feel that the authorities should attempt to legislate morality, or do you feel that this should be left up to the discretion of the individuals involved?

*A:* I don't believe that the government has any business legislating morality. But we live in a nation that has traditionally legislated morals, and to leave a vacuum in this area would be a tacit approval, so I'm caught between a rock and a hard place.

*Q:* What is your opinion of the "Moral Majority" movement among fundamentalists?

*A:* This reflects back to the answer above. As long as we are going to make laws concerning it, I feel that the Christian position has as much right to be heard as any other position. The Gay Libbers are not opposed to fostering their views, and that has an effect on the legislative process. The way I look at it is that since the homosexual lifestyle is such a dominant factor in the life of homosexuals, and since it is an option and not mandatory, and because of the strong influence it has on others with whom they come in contact, there are certain privileges—not rights—that should be denied these people. It is not a right to teach school; it is a privilege. Also, public school is supported by the taxpayers. For example, I have two kids in school, and since I'm locked up in here I can't be with them to teach them my values. I wouldn't want them to be taught by an effeminate homosexual. They might identify with him and adopt his values or characteristics, and this is not what I want for my kids. I see the educational issue as the crucial issue.

### Interview with Christian Inmate #3

*Q:* Do you feel that a homosexual act between consenting adults is wrong?

*A:* Whether they are consenting or not, in my opinion it's wrong. When you are a Christian you go by the Word of God and the Bible says that in the last days, and we believe these to be the last days, that the people will become lovers of their own selves and people of pleasure who pursue their own lust. If we go to the Bible we can see that God's plan for man was set forth in the Garden of Eden when God created woman as man's helpmate and companion. Being Christians we seek to operate according to God's standards and God speaks out strongly against homosexuality.

*Q:* What do you think causes people to become homosexuals?

*A:* A lack of authority in the home, especially as delegated by the father; lack of a proper male role model; and also just plain lust. I believe people have a choice in the matter. I don't believe people are born with homosexual tendencies.

*Q:* Do you feel that homosexuals should be granted full legal and social rights?

*A:* I feel that all people should have the same rights, but we should not only consider the rights of the people who are pressing for change but we should consider the rights of the people that might be affected. People should have the right to determine who their children will be influenced by.

*Q:* Do you feel that homosexual acts between consenting adults should be illegal?

*A:* Yes. The only rights we have are the rights the Lord gives us.

*Q:* Do you think that homosexual inmates have a harder time in prison than heterosexual inmates due to pressure and discrimination?

*A:* Yes, I think they do.

*Q:* Do you feel that the prison should do more or less in the way of protecting homosexual inmates?

*A:* The question arises in my mind "Do homosexual inmates need protection?" When someone comes to me for counseling and says "I'm being pressured" or "They're trying to turn 'em out," I say, "Well, stand up for your rights, fight back." I know this might sound strange coming from a minister, but if we are right we should stand up for them.

*Q:* Do you agree that the MCC should be allowed to come and conduct services for homosexuals here in prison?

*A:* That's a real loaded question. I would say that as long as MCC is helpful to the inmates that they should be allowed the services. As long as they preach sound biblical doctrine, I would agree. But I do disagree with the MCC justifying their homosexuality by the Word of

God. I do believe that we should show 100% Christian love to the MCC in hopes that love will minister to them.

Q: Do you believe that masturbation is wrong?

A: There is no specific scipture in the Bible that says that it is wrong, point blank. But since our body is the temple of the Holy Spirit, we should not defile it. People who do masturbate who are Christians walking in the Spirit of the Lord know immediately, after the act, that it is wrong.

Q: Do you believe that premarital intercourse between a man and woman is wrong, if they love each other?

A: Yes, I believe it is wrong. It is biblically wrong and against God's plan for man whether they love each other or not.

Q: Do you think that sexual activity between inmates is very common here in prison?

A: I really don't even know the answer to that. I'm not that close to inmate relationships.

Q: Do you think that forced or pressured encounters are very common here in prison?

A: That's another hard one. As for *very* common, I'd say no. As far as common, I'd have to say yes.

Q: In society in general do you feel that the authorities should attempt to legislate morality, or do you feel that this should be left up to the discretion of the individuals involved?

A: I feel that the U.S. government should be under God ethically as it was designed to be in the Constitution.

Q: What is your opinion of the "Moral Majority" movement among fundamentalists?

A: I've seen some things that I didn't agree with in the movement, such as a lack of love toward homosexuals and criminals, et cetera. But I believe that they could be very influential in getting the country back on its feet. I don't believe that anybody should attempt to force their views on anybody else, but I don't see the Moral Majority as forcing their views. There's a difference between making your views known and forcing them.

## Interview with Muslim Inmate #1

Q: Do you feel that a homosexual act between consenting adults is wrong?

A: I feel that it is unnatural. There's nothing productive that comes of it.

*Q:* What do you think causes people to become homosexual?

*A:* It is the fault of their parents and the way that they raised them. In our society people have not learned to be proper parents. I believe that parents are very important in shaping the proper values and behavior in their children. I do not believe it is due to genetic or biological causes.

*Q:* Do you feel that homosexuals should be granted full legal and social rights?

*A:* Yes.

*Q:* Do you feel that homosexual acts between consenting adults should be illegal?

*A:* I don't believe that it should be legislated against.

*Q:* Do you think that homosexual inmates have a harder time in prison than heterosexual inmates due to pressure and discrimination?

*A:* No. It really depends on the maturity of the person. I've seen some homosexuals who have it better, and then I've seen some who have a lot of problems. It really depends on the individual.

*Q:* Do you feel that the prison should do more or less in the way of protecting homosexual inmates?

*A:* I don't believe in segregating certain groups. I don't believe that they should do any more for one group of people than another. They should make every effort to protect everyone who is in their custody.

*Q:* Do you agree that the MCC should be allowed to come and conduct services for homosexuals here in prison?

*A:* Yes. Everybody should have their religious freedom.

*Q:* Do you believe that masturbation is wrong?

*A:* No.

*Q:* Do you believe that premarital intercourse between a man and woman is wrong, if they love each other?

*A:* I believe it is wrong. You should be married before you engage in sex, especially if there's a chance of children.

*Q:* Do you think that sexual activity between inmates is very common here in prison?

*A:* I'd have to say no. I hear people talking about it, but I really don't have any firsthand knowledge of it.

*Q:* Do you think that forced or pressured encounters are very common here in prison?

*A:* No.

*Q:* In society in general, do you feel that the authorities should attempt to legislate morality, or do you feel that this should be left up to the discretion of the individuals involved?

*A:* It should be left up to the individual. It's the parent's place to instill the proper morals.

*Q:* What is your opinion of the "Moral Majority" movement among fundamentalists? What is your standard of morality?

*A:* I use the Koran scriptures, but the essence of truth or right is within each person. However, it may be clouded over by faulty upbringing.'

# 10

# Staff Attitudes toward Homosexuality

Before 1970 prison policy dictated that any inmate found guilty of a "sexual conduct" violation automatically received twenty-eight evenings and four weekends "confined to quarters" (CTQ). As we point out in the next chapter, there has been a drastic liberalizing of this policy in this prison since then. Today the punishment is left to the descretion of the hearing officer who reviews the citation reports filed by the correctional officers.

As was clear from our interviews with the homosexuals in prison, the general consensus among them was that the attitudes and norms of the convict appear not to have improved since the convict continues to disrespect and exploit them. On another note, the homosexuals questioned and interviewed did report a more liberal attitude among many of the staff.

Any changes in attitudes and behavior with respect to prison sexual exploitation among inmates are quite subtle. Generally speaking, those inmates who appear to be more sensitive to the homosexuals are the college student group, the better educated, the older men, and certain participants

in "PCP" (peer counseling program, involving group therapy). The vast majority of the convict population—especially those men who shape and maintain the prison sexual
code—are not sensitive to the feelings of the men who are
exploited. These convicts may know that a situation is not
right, but they tend not to care. If they see an attractive
youngster or homosexual, they do not think about right or
wrong. If they see something they want, they merely take
it. The more sensitive and concerned individuals, even if
they were in the majority, would not change anything
because they do not have the power. As the saying goes,
"Muscle runs the joints, not brains."

With respect to the prison staff, on the other hand,
there is some evidence of greater sensitivity toward and
concern for inmates who are victims of sexual harassment.
This sensitivity was noted and appreciated by many of our
homosexual respondents (35%). These attitudinal changes
are primarily reflected on an individual level, however,
and do not reflect changes among all the prison personnel
or in prison policy or administrative procedure. As stated
in several of the following interviews, the liberalizing of
attitudes that has occurred results from the fact that society
at large has increased its awareness about homosexuals and
has generally become more supportive of improving the
social conditions for homosexual people. In this sense the
liberalization by staff members toward homosexuals and
homosexuality reflects the liberalizing trends emergent in
the early to mid-1970s. As we discuss in the next chapter,
however, the country is turning politically and ideologi-
cally to the right and these conservative trends may usher
in less liberal views on this issue.

To understand the attitudes of the prison staff toward
homosexuality, eight of twenty correctional officers
assigned to different shifts in one building were contacted
to be interviewed. Only one tier officer refused to be inter-

viewed. As the seven interviews will show, the attitudes of most of the staff members interviewed reflect a somewhat lenient approach toward homosexuality. Although one officer disapproved of homosexuality and held attitudes that could be considered as homophobic, the other officers interviewed recognized that homosexuality was a reality in prison life and indicated that they were concerned about the exploitation of homosexuals and vulnerable youngsters.

We should point out that the officers interviewed here are those considered most approachable by the co-author, and do not reflect an accurate consensus of the views and attitudes of the majority of the staff.

Because these interviews substantiate the perceptions of greater staff sensitivity and staff support of homosexuals being hooked up reported by the homosexuals in our survey, we present the interviews in their entirety as we believe these more permissive attitudes are quite unique in a prison environment. Many of the prisoners also indicated their surprise at finding some of the staff to be as lenient and supportive as they were. Staff attitudes in the hard-core prisons tend to be quite different.

INTERVIEW WITH CORRECTIONAL OFFICER #1

*Q:* How long have you been a correctional officer?
*A:* Nine years.
*Q:* Have you worked at any other institutions?
*A:* Chino and here two years.
*Q:* Do you feel that homosexual acts between consenting adults are wrong?
*A:* No.
*Q:* Do you feel that homosexuals should have full legal rights?
*A:* Yes.
*Q:* On approximately how many occasions have you written 115s for sexual conduct?

A: Probably around ten a year, mostly while I was at Chino where I worked for seven years. Here, I haven't written any.

Q: Do you agree that sexual conduct between *consenting* inmates should be classified as a serious 115?

A: Yes. It's not fair for homosexuals to be allowed to have sex when the heterosexual inmates cannot have it. I think it would probably take some of the thrill out of it for some of them [homosexuals] if it were legal. Also, it's hard to tell whether it is forced or not.

Q: Do you think that sexual activity is very common here in prison?

A: I don't know. I haven't been here long enough.

Q: Do you think that forced or pressured sexual encounters are very common?

A: That's true. I'm sure it is. It certainly was elsewhere.

Q: According to your own personal values and beliefs, do you make any distinction between the active and the passive partner?

A: No, I don't make any distinction. They are both breaking the rule.

Q: Do you think that homosexual inmates have a more difficult time in prison than heterosexual inmates, due to pressure and discrimination?

A: A large majority of them do have a more difficult time. Not just for the queens who are most subject to pressure, but also for the jockers who must cope with the psychological pressures of staying undercover and maintaining "face" in front of their friends. [Note: Our observations and data do not support this observation. On the contrary, the jockers are open about their relationships and there is no social stigma attached.]

Q: It seems to me that to a degree the staff seems to tolerate and even encourage sexual relationships between inmates in that they will move two inmates onto a tier together, et cetera.

A: To a degree this is true. It's a way of keeping down trouble and maintaining order. Also it cuts down on the paperwork. If two people are hooked up and living on different tiers or in different buildings, then they are going to be constantly out of bounds and creating problems for the tier officers. It's easier to overlook or downplay sexual conduct if they both live on the same tier.

Q: How do you view the above in light of the fact that sexual conduct is a violation of the rules? It seems they are saying "Go ahead, just don't get caught."

A: Basically that's a true statement.

Q: Do you feel that homosexual inmates should be sent to the softer joints, and screened out of the hard-core institutions such as San Quentin, et cetera?

A: That is a very complex problem because there are many different criteria to be considered—his custody classification, whether he is violent or aggressive, the type of crime he was committed for. Perhaps he's the type who can't hold up under pressure and reacts violently or aggressively. I think they can do more than they do now. Definitely the system does create some of the problems. Much of it depends on the individual case. One thing is that they don't have the opportunity at the reception centers to really observe and evaluate each individual. What they tend to look at mostly is the paperwork. I think that they should have counselors working in the housing units observing the men and how they react, and they should have some input into the classification process rather than just some counselor sitting at a desk making these decisions on the basis of a ten-minute interview.

Q: Do you think it is a very common occurrence for young straight boys to be turned out, or forced into being punks?

A: Yes, however some of them allow it to happen. They use it as a ploy to gain their own ends for candy or cigarettes, or to stay at a particular institution.

Q: Do you feel that this prison should give more priority to screening out the young passive inmates, straight or gay, and placing them in the softer institutions?

A: Yes, they should.

Q: What changes, if any, have you seen in prison policies, written or unwritten, toward homosexuals over the years?

A: No, I haven't seen any change at all. There are a lot more homosexuals now than there used to be, at least outfront homosexuals.

Q: Do you feel that homosexual inmates per se pose any more of a threat to the security or order of the institution than heterosexual inmates?

A: Some homosexual inmates are a problem; some are not; some are a constant problem. At Chino some of them were very emotionally immature, and totally promiscuous. They did not use good sense or show any type of descretion; they just created problems for themselves. For example, they would get in a lover's quarrel and run back and slash their wrists, and the next day they would be right back involved in the same old game over again.

Q: Have you found any one race more prone to engage in prison sexual conduct than the others?

A: Not really. In many rapes blacks do tend to be the aggressors. I think it's because of the physical size and power of the blacks. Most of them work out and are big, and as a group they appear to be more threatening and intimidating, whereas the whites are just a bunch of scuzzy bikers, and the Mexicans tend to stick more to their own race. Somehow they don't seem as threatening as the blacks.

Q: Being that a sexual act between inmates is a legally prosecutable felony, why is it that they are never referred to the D.A. for prosecution?

A: It's just not worth it—plus the fact that society as a whole is changing attitudes toward it. It's too much paperwork.

Q: Is there any statement you would like to add to this study?

A: I feel that those homosexuals who want to should be allowed to live in any wing or tier they can get along on. However, there should be segregated housing provided for those who need or want it. At Chino all "flamboyant" homosexuals are placed in segregated housing.

## INTERVIEW WITH CORRECTIONAL OFFICER #2

Q: How long have you have a correctional officer?

A: Five years at a state mental hospital as a psychiatric technician and seven years here.

Q: Do you feel that homosexual acts between consenting adults are wrong?

A: I don't think it is natural, but I don't condemn anybody for doing it. I don't pass value judgments. I'm somewhere between calling it an alternative lifestyle and calling it an aberration.

Q: Do you feel that homosexuals should be given full legal and social rights?

A: Yes.

Q: On approximately how many occasions have you written 115s for sexual conduct?

A: Over the years, fifty to seventy-five times. It used to be that I wrote one or two a month. Now that I am on day shift, maybe one or two a year.

Q: Do you agree that sexual conduct between *consenting* inmates should be classified as a serious 115?

A: No, not as long as it is mutually consenting. I can't think of any instances where anything serious has come of it.

Q: Do you think that sexual activity is very common here in prison?

A: Yes.

Q: Do you think that forced or pressured sexual encounters are very common?

*A:* Yes, but not as much as in the county jails. I would say that maybe 25% of the [sexual] encounters are for nonaffectional reasons—some for commissary, and some due to pressure of varying degrees. Outright physical rape is probably less common.

*Q:* According to your own personal values and beliefs, do you make any distinction between the active and the passive partner?

*A:* No.

*Q:* Do you think that homosexual inmates have a more difficult time in prison than heterosexual inmates due to pressure and discrimination?

*A:* Yes, they have to contend with problems that heterosexuals don't have to. However, at this facility it's minimal compared to some of the others.

*Q:* It seems to me that to a degree the staff seems to tolerate and even encourage sexual relationships between inmates in that they will move two inmates onto a tier together, et cetera.

*A:* Institutional policy is definitely against it. The lieutenant's position is that he doesn't want all of the homosexuals on the same tier. He doesn't want all bikers on the same tier and he doesn't want all Christians housed together. They try to disperse them throughout the institution. It may happen informally. There may be exceptions made, but these happen on a level of which I am not aware.

*Q:* How do you view the above in view of the fact that sexual conduct is a violation of the rules? It seems they are saying "Go ahead, just don't get caught."

*A:* I don't agree, at least not as a matter of policy.

*Q:* Do you feel that homosexual inmates should be sent to the softer joints, and screened out of the hard-core institutions such as San Quentin, et cetera?

*A:* That is a controversial issue they are wrestling with right now. Did you know that? The issue is whether to randomly distribute the people throughout the institutions, or whether to classify them according to background and behavioral characteristics and try and place certain types in certain institutions. I personally believe they should make every effort to be sensitive to the circumstances and needs of the individuals. It seems that one of the drawbacks to this job is that you tend to become very hard and cynical. It callouses you to human concerns. They have policies covering this sort of thing. They should follow the policies they have.

*Q:* Do you think it is a very common occurrence for young straight boys to be turned out, or forced into being punks?

A: It probably happens a lot more than is known. Most people don't want to be labeled as snitches. I think county jails have a lot higher incidences. Probably a lot of the forced sexual encounters are the result of low-key pressure and nonviolent rape, as opposed to actual violent assault.

Q: What changes, if any, have you seen in prison policies, written or unwritten, toward homosexuals over the years?

A: When I started we had no inmate appeal procedures or provisions for investigative officer reports. Everybody was found guilty. The inmate's side of the story never made any difference. The standard punishment was twenty-eight plus four—twenty-eight evenings plus four weekends lockup. This was about 1969 to 1971. It used to be almost a game like hunting, back then, to catch sexual conduct. Back then we used to catch two or three a week; now it's more like one or two a month on night shift.

Q: Do you feel that homosexual inmates per se pose any more of a threat to the security or order of the institution than heterosexual inmates?

A: No.

Q: Have you found any one race more prone to engage in prison sexual conduct than the others?

A: Not that I can tell. I don't really know what it is like from the inmates' standpoint, so I can only guess.

Q: Being that a sexual act between inmates is a legally prosecutable felony, why is it that they are never referred to the D.A. for prosecution?

A: It's hard to document. The court requires proof of penetration. The officer must actually observe penetration, which is hard to do. If two inmates are in a room doing it and the officer keys the door, by the time the door is open they are shifted around. Also, it's an evolutionary thing. It's more of a reflection of society. I think nowadays homosexuality is such an outfront issue it would be ludicrous for a jury to find a guy guilty of a felony just for sexual activity.


## INTERVIEW WITH CORRECTIONAL OFFICER #3

Q: How long have you been a correctional officer?

A: Eighteen years.

Q: Have you worked at any other institutions?

A: Yes, minimum security; no maximum security.

Q: Do you feel that homosexual acts between consenting adults are wrong?

*A:* Yes.

*Q:* Do you feel that homosexuals should be given full legal and social rights?

*A:* No, perhaps in some cases if they conduct themselves properly and don't try to publicize their preferences or to force the issue. Psychiatrists and sociologists are out screwing up other people's minds. Why shouldn't homosexuals.

*Q:* Do you agree that sexual conduct between *consenting* inmates should be classified as a serious 115?

*A:* Yes.

*Q:* Do you think that sexual activity is very common here in prison?

*A:* Sorry to say, yes.

*Q:* Do you think that forced or pressured sexual encounters are very common?

*A:* Yes.

*Q:* According to your own personal values and beliefs, do you make any distinction between the active and the passive partner?

*A:* No.

*Q:* Do you think that homosexual inmates have a more difficult time in prison than heterosexual inmates due to pressure and discrimination?

*A:* In some cases.

*Q:* It seems to me that to a degree the staff seems to tolerate and even encourage sexual relationships between inmates in that they will move two inmates onto a tier together, et cetera.

*A:* No, definitely not.

*Q:* Do you feel that homosexual inmates should be sent to the softer joints, and screened out of the hard-core institutions such as San Quentin, et cetera.

*A:* Well, look at it this way. How much money do you think the taxpayers are willing to spend? Nobody asked these people to come here. They worked very hard to get in here.

*Q:* Do you think it is a very common occurrence for young straight boys to be turned out, or forced into being punks?

*A:* Yes, but not as common as some people would like to have the public believe.

*Q:* What changes, if any, have you seen in prison policies, written or unwritten, toward homosexuals over the years?

*A:* The policies have not changed. However, the staff is more tolerant and accepting of homosexuals than they used to be.

*Q:* Do you feel that homosexual inmates per se pose any more of a threat to the security or order of the institution than heterosexual inmates?

*A:* Less of a security threat.

*Q:* Have you found any one race more prone to engage in prison sexual conduct than the others?

*A:* No.

*Q:* Being that a sexual act between inmates is a legally prosecutable felony, why is it that they are never referred to the D.A. for prosecution?

*A:* Has to do with the greater tolerance in society in general.

## Interview with Correctional Officer #4

*Q:* How long have you been a correctional officer?

*A:* Eleven and a half years.

*Q:* Have you worked at any other institutions?

*A:* Yes, Vacaville.

*Q:* Do you feel that homosexual acts between consenting adults are wrong?

*A:* No, as long as no force is involved.

*Q:* Do you feel that homosexuals should be given full legal and social rights?

*A:* Yes, with exceptions, as long as they don't try to force their feelings on others.

*Q:* On approximately how many occasions have you written 115s for sexual conduct?

*A:* None.

*Q:* Do you agree that sexual conduct between *consenting* inmates should be classified as a serious 115?

*A:* Yes, due to possible violent repercussions, due to jealousies, et cetera.

*Q:* Do you think that sexual activity is very common here in prison?

*A:* Yes.

*Q:* Do you think that forced or pressured sexual encounters are very common?

*A:* Yes.

*Q:* According to your own personal values and beliefs, do you make any distinction between the active and the passive partner?

*A:* No.

*Q:* Do you think that homosexual inmates have a more difficult time in prison than heterosexual inmates due to pressure and discrimination?

*A:* Yes.

Q: It seems to me that to a degree the staff seems to tolerate and even encourage sexual relationships between inmates in that they will move two inmates onto a tier together, et cetera.

A: I do not feel that the staff covertly encourages relationships between inmates. However, they do more or less take the attitude of "out of sight, out of mind."

Q: How do you view the above in view of the fact that sexual conduct is a violation of the rules? It seems they are saying "Go ahead, just don't get caught."

A: To a degree this is true. Why worry about it as long as you don't catch them?

Q: Do you feel that homosexual inmates should be sent to the softer joints, and screened out of the hard-core institutions such as San Quentin, et cetera?

A: That poses a lot of problems. How do you decide who is and who isn't [a homosexual]? I think many inmates may try to use it to avoid being sent to the hard-core joints.

Q: Do you think it is a very common occurrence for young straight boys to be turned out, or forced into being punks?

A: Yes, I'm sure it happens.

Q: What changes, if any, have you seen in prison policies, written or unwritten, toward homosexuals over the years?

A: No policy change, some loosening of attitudes.

Q: Do you feel that homosexual inmates per se pose any more of a threat to the security or order of the institution than heterosexual inmates?

A: Not by themselves, but due to the attitudes of the general population.

Q: Have you found any one race more prone to engage in prison sexual conduct than the others?

A: Chicanos, less prone.

Q: Being that a sexual act between inmates is a legally prosecutable felony, why is it that they are never referred to the D.A. for prosecution?

A: The system does not want the publicity, it does not want the public's attention called to the issue. Also, I feel that the courts would ultimately deem the activity as not illegal, considering the state law concerning consenting adults.

Q: Is there any statement you would like to add to this study?

A: I think that the administration could do more to control the situation and alleviate the problems faced by weak individuals, but I am not sure what should be done. I do feel that the administration tends to keep the identities of homosexual inmates from their tier officer, and I think this hinders the officers from effectively performing their job. [Interviewer asked why this is.] Because they [the administrators] don't have confidence in the officers. They are afraid that the officers may identify the homosexuals to the other inmates.

## Interview with Correctional Officer #5

Q: How long have you been a correctional officer?
A: Four years.
Q: Have you worked at any other institutions?
A: Folsom for two years, here for two years.
Q: Do you feel that homosexual acts between consenting adults are wrong?
A: No.
Q: Do you feel that homosexuals should be given full legal and social rights?
A: No, at least no position of authority or influence over minors. [Interviewer asked why.] Because people in authority should have the respect of others, and in the social climate as it is today I don't think most people respect homosexuals. Right or wrong, that's just the way it is.
Q: On approximately how many occasions have you written 115s for sexual conduct?
A: Once.
Q: Do you agree that sexual conduct between *consenting* inmates should be classified as a serious 115?
A: Yes.
Q: Do you think that sexual activity is very common here in prison?
A: Yes.
Q: Do you think that forced or pressured sexual encounters are very common?
A: It is not rare, but I don't think it is an everyday occurrence.
Q: According to your own personal values and beliefs, do you make any distinction between the active and the passive partner?
A: No.
Q: Do you think that homosexual inmates have a more difficult time in prison than heterosexual inmates due to pressure and discrimination?
A: Of course they have a tougher time.

*Q:* It seems to me that to a degree the staff seems to tolerate and even encourage sexual relationships between inmates in that they will move two inmates onto a tier together, et cetera.

*A:* Not the line officers, but perhaps the administration. I have had a situation where a homosexual has come to me, her jocker was living on my tier, and she asked if it would be okay for her to move onto my tier. She assured me that there would be no problems, so I agreed, and they didn't cause any problems.

*Q:* How do you view the above in view of the fact that sexual conduct is a violation of the rules? It seems they are saying "Go ahead, just don't get caught."

*A:* It's a "Catch 22" situation. If you're going to do it, don't get caught. It's like the father telling his unmarried daughter, "don't do it, but if you do, be sure and take precautions."

*Q:* Do you feel that homosexual inmates should be sent to the softer joints, and screened out of the hard-core joints such as San Quentin?

*A:* Yes, they should. It is a matter of time and manpower. The case loads are heavy and people tend to get sloppy. The policy guidelines are there, but sometimes they aren't followed as closely as they should be.

*Q:* Do you think it is a very common occurrence for young straight boys to be turned out, or forced into being punks?

*A:* Yes.

*Q:* What changes, if any, have you seen in prison policies, written or unwritten, toward homosexuals over the years?

*A:* It has become more lenient. I think the enforcement of the sexual conduct rules is slacking and will soon fall by the wayside. [Interviewer asked why.] Because the whole society is becoming more liberal.

*Q:* Do you feel that homosexual inmates per se pose any more of a threat to the security or order of the institution than heterosexual inmates?

*A:* No.

*Q:* Have you found any one race more prone to engage in prison sexual conduct than the others?

*A:* I would say that blacks and whites are about equal and Mexicans somewhat less.

*Q:* Being that a sexual act between inmates is a legally prosecutable felony, why is it that they are never referred to the D.A. for prosecution?

*A:* Because they don't rate the D.A.'s priority.

INTERVIEW WITH CORRECTIONAL OFFICER #6 (FEMALE)

Q: How long have you been a correctional officer?
A: Five years.
Q: Have you worked at any other institutions?
A: Men's Colony four and a half years, here six months.
Q: Do you feel that homosexual acts between consenting adults are wrong?
A: No.
Q: Do you feel that homosexuals should be given full legal and social rights?
A: Yes.
Q: On approximately how many occasions have you written 115s for sexual conduct?
A: Never.
Q: Do you agree that sexual conduct between *consenting* inmates should be classified as a serious 115?
A: I really don't know about that one. It would be like allowing common law conjugal visits; some gal might come up and visit one guy one month and another one the next, and it could cause fights. Another problem would be in determining whether both partners were really consenting or not.
Q: Do you think that sexual activity is very common here in prison?
A: Yes.
Q: Do you think that forced or pressured sexual encounters are very common?
A: Yes, but not that much.
Q: According to your own personal values and beliefs, do you make any distinction between the active and the passive partner?
A: No.
Q: Do you think that homosexual inmates have a more difficult time in prison than heterosexual inmates due to pressure and discrimination?
A: I think that it would depend on the individual. Many do, definitely.
Q: It seems to me that to a degree the staff seems to tolerate and even encourage sexual relationships between inmates in that they will move two inmates onto a tier together, et cetera.
A: I'll say tolerate, but not encourage. I've seen room moves squashed for the same reason.
Q: How do you view the above in view of the fact that sexual conduct

is a violation of the rules? It seems they are saying "Go ahead, just don't get caught."

A: I can't really agree with that because I know a lot of officers who really try to bust them.

Q: Do you feel that homosexual inmates should be sent to the softer joints, and screened out of the hard-core joints such as San Quentin?

A: Definitely yes, straight or gay, definitely.

Q: Do you think it is a very common occurrence for young straight boys to be turned out, or forced into being punks?

A: I don't want to say *very* common, but I would say it is common.

Q: What changes, if any, have you seen in prison policies, written or unwritten, toward homosexuals over the years?

A: I haven't really seen any changes in the policies. In other joints on the main line, they couldn't be outfront; they are here. They couldn't dress and wear makeup. However, they did allow it in the P.C. [Protective Custody] wing.

Q: Have you found any one race more prone to engage in prison sexual conduct than the others?

A: No, not really.

Q: Being that a sexual act between inmates is a legally prosecutable felony, why is it that they are never referred to the D.A. for prosecution?

A: Probably because the D.A. wouldn't take it. That's just my opinion. They're too busy to sweat something that isn't that serious. There's more important things.

## Interview with Correctional Officer #7

Q: How long have you been a correctional officer?

A: Seven years.

Q: Have you worked at any other institutions?

A: Tracy for five years, here for two years.

Q: Do you feel that homosexual acts between consenting adults are wrong?

A: No.

Q: Do you feel that homosexuals should be given full legal and social rights?

A: No. My primary concern is the influence it might have on my family. Other than that, I am not concerned. I feel that things like this which young people are exposed to can leave imprints and affect their minds for years and years. Just so you'll get some idea where I am coming from, I was brought up in a strict fundamentalist church. I wasn't even aware that there was such a thing as a homosexual until I was about eighteen years old.

*Q:* On approximately how many occasions have you written 115s for sexual conduct?

*A:* I truly don't remember writing any. I haven't caught anybody in the act. I haven't even caught two inmates in a cell together naked.

*Q:* Do you agree that sexual conduct between *consenting* inmates should be classified as a serious 115?

*A:* It depends on the nature of the sexual conduct. If you catch two inmates in a cell and you don't actually see them in the act, then it should be an "administrative" 115. If you catch them committing a sexual act, it should be classified "serious," pending investigation. If it is truly consenting, it should not be serious. But how can you be sure it is really mutually consenting, and that the person is not just saying so because of pressure or threat from the other party?

*Q:* Do you think that sexual activity is very common here in prison?

*A:* I would say that probably the majority of inmates engage in sexual activity, at least sometimes. But I don't think they do it every day, or even three or four times a week.

*Q:* Do you think that forced or pressured sexual encounters are very common?

*A:* I would say less here. Where I worked before, a prison which houses twelve hundred inmates, we were averaging five rapes a month. [Interviewer asked if there was a interracial component involved.] I would say about 5% involved black aggressors and white victims. The racial gangs wouldn't have tolerated much more of it without major racial trouble.

*Q:* According to your own personal values and beliefs, do you make any distinction between the active and the passive partner?

*A:* No, I feel they are both homosexual. The pitcher may be more bisexual.

*Q:* Do you think that homosexual inmates have a more difficult time in prison than heterosexual inmates due to pressure and intimidation?

*A:* That's a yes and no question. I'd say they would have more problems than the jockers and they would have less problems than the young, weak straight inmates. The homosexuals are more equipped psychologically to handle it. The young straight kid is either going to get out there and buff a lot of iron or he's going to get turned out.

*Q:* It seems to me that to a degree the staff seems to tolerate and even encourage sexual relationships between inmates in that they will move two inmates onto a tier together, et cetera.

*A:* I'd say that's definitely true at this institution. Keep in mind that's a management-level decision at the level of lieutenant or above.

*Q:* How do you view the above in view of the fact that sexual conduct is a violation of the rules? It seems they are saying "Go ahead, just don't get caught."

*A:* I agree with that. In fact, I've been told this by some of my supervisors—that they're not really that concerned. That's here at this institution. In the maximum-security prisons it's different. The main things they're concerned about here is shanks, hard narcotics, and pruno, because of their violent nature.

*Q:* Do you feel that homosexual inmates should be sent to the softer joints and screened out of the hard-core joints such as San Quentin?

*A:* They already are. At Tracy, anytime we caught anybody who started plucking his eyebrows or was an outfront queen, he was immediately put on the bus to this prison. Homosexuals are basically no problem. They are not usually a violent-type inmate, and therefore they have an easier time qualifying for an easier type of institution. I don't feel that any first-termers should be subjected to an institution like San Quentin or Soledad unless they have a lot of Y.A. [Youth Authority] time or numerous county jail sentences, or unless they are extremely violent.

*Q:* Do you think it is a very common occurrence for young straight boys to be turned out, or forced into being punks?

*A:* That just depends on the institution and it depends on the person. If the guy can fight and is willing to get down, then nine times out of ten he won't get raped. It's all a matter of physical stature and looks. The guy has to be willing to get a pipe or shank and defend himself. [See our note at end of the interview.]

*Q:* Do you feel that this prison should give more priority to screening out the young passive inmates, straight or gay, and placing them in the softer institutions?

*A:* Any young guy that gets sent to D.V.I. [Deuel Vocational Institute] or San Quentin is going to get raped. They are going to get raped or they are going to carry a shank or something and be willing to fight for it. It's either fight or fuck. If the person doesn't submit, if he fights and picks up a piece, he's going to wind up in a gang and then it's all downhill from there—stabbings, narcotics, et cetera. Gangs are the largest contributing factor to recidivism. Once they adopt the hard-core attitude that they aren't going to take any shit from anybody and take it out onto the streets, it brings them right back to prison. Recidivism rate at Soledad is probably around 90% whereas here it's probably 50 or 60%.

Q: What changes, if any, have you seen in prison policies, written or unwritten, toward homosexuals over the years?

A: I haven't seen any at all. At the other prison, we didn't have as many homosexuals as we do here, so I can't really say.

Q: Do you feel that homosexual inmates per se pose any more of a threat to the security or order of the institution than heterosexual inmates?

A: No, in fact I would say that they help because they are basically passive.

Q: Have you found any one race more prone to engage in prison sexual conduct than the others?

A: No, I feel that the Orientals engage in less, but they are more prone to being raped due to their small stature and numbers.

Q: Being that a sexual act between inmates is a legally prosecutable felony, why is it that they are never referred to the D.A. for prosecution?

A: The only thing that I've been told is that it is difficult in obtaining prosecution.

Note: We do not feel that defending himself in this way is a viable alternative for the heterosexual youngster. Possession or use of any weapon within prison is a serious felony offense which is rigorously prosecuted within the local jurisdiction. In addition, institutional disciplinary policy demands that a convict who uses weapons while in custody be confined to long-term lockdown in isolation, and it often results in his being transferred to a "Control Unit" at a maximum-security institution for the time remaining on his sentence.

# 11

## Prison Policy, Programs, and Change

The patterns of sexual exploitation and sexual behavior documented by our study are *not* new patterns. According to historian Jonathan Katz, the earliest recorded observance of sexual victimization and activity in a penal institution was, in fact, a letter dated April 12, 1826.[27] In that account, written by a layman to a public official, the author argued for the improvement of prison conditions for those inmates who had been "prostituted to the lust of old convicts." Over 150 years later the situation in prison appears to be relatively unchanged (and unchallenged).

Although the issue of prison sexuality is complex, by focusing on exploitation we have attempted to describe the prison sexual scene in one prison as it affects both the victim and the victimizer. And although we have pointed to a greater sensitivity on the part of some staff members toward the fate of the homosexuals and vulnerable heterosexual youngsters, sexual exploitation remains a reality of prison life. Because we feel that this continued pattern is detrimental to the individuals involved as well as to the penal institution itself, in this concluding chapter we raise several important issues and concerns. *Our underlying goal and philosophy is to work toward improving the conditions in prison so that inmates can be rehabilitated; and, we contend, a climate of sexual victimization and exploitation is not conducive to rehabilitation.*

## PRISON POLICY AND CHANGE

According to our discussions with the policy deputy director of the State of California Department of Corrections (CDC), the department began in 1981 to implement a new system of inmate classification which is based on a scoring device designed to indicate the level of security required for each prisoner. The objective of this new system was to send each person received at one of the two statewide reception centers to an institution or camp matching the inmate's classification score. Accordingly, the policy of the department is for the placement of inmates at the lowest practical security level of housing commensurate with housing availability and individual program needs.

To implement this new policy, the department has designated four distinct security levels which are directly related to physical control needs. These levels are: *Level I* is the lowest security level and includes nonsecure housing consisting of either dormitories or individual rooms/cells surrounded by an indirectly supervised perimeter or without a secure perimeter; *Level II* is a slightly more restrictive form of Level I housing with a more secure and constantly supervised perimeter; *Level III* requires secure single-person-cell housing, an armed perimeter, and controlled inmate movement; and *Level IV* is the most restrictive of the four security levels in which housing configurations are single-person-cells with armed capability inside, the perimeter is armed, and inmate movement is restricted.[28]

In this new placement system, those "known" homosexuals and vulnerable youngsters ("immature inmates") are usually placed in Level III, although quite often, according to the deputy director, their crime, demeanor, and prison behavior do *not* warrant such a secure level of housing. The difficulty in placing these men in lower-level security is that in the past the rangers running the conservation camps (Level I) have not wanted these "types" of inmates, and the dormitory settings (Level II) have promoted sexual coercion and activity.

Furthermore, according to this policy-maker, in the later 1950s when the CDC decided to concentrate the homosexuals in one penal institution and building, the authorities found that these men immediately stratified themselves, with the more aggressive of the group coming to control the weaker in a manner similar to what had been happening when they had been dispersed throughout the penal system. Because of this experience the deputy director did not support the separation of homosexuals from the general prison population.

This official did feel, however, that the situation might improve in the future with the building of new penal facilities. According to current plans, the new prisons to be built in the state will house from 2000 to 2500 inmates in four or five 500-bed units. Each of these units will be further broken down into 16-bed or 48-bed clusters. These separate clusters will allow the officials to assign housing to groups such as the homosexuals and the kids requiring specialized attention and programs. In the meantime, according to the official, the situation remains critical due to overcrowding and due to the fact that it is too expensive to remodel or change any of the existing facilities.

Before the implementation of this new placement policy, the CDC had a placement policy which specified the placement procedures separating the homosexuals and vulnerable heterosexual youngsters from the aggressive heterosexuals. But *in reality*—as our study has shown—these different types of men were neither consistently assigned to particular penal institutions nor were they separated by designated areas within each institution.

PRISON PLACEMENT PRACTICES

As previously stated, when possible the state placement board tries to assign the effeminate homosexuals to an institution which has separate, nondormitory housing so as to lessen the incidence of both sexual activity and sexual assault. Such placement, however, is based in large measure on the availability of a certain type of housing (a single-man cell) at the time of the inmate's entry into the penal system. Even with the planned addition of 2000 beds by 1985, according to the deputy director, the CDC anticipates being short 9000 beds.

The earlier *Classification Manual* specified that inmates were to be sent to this prison under study if they had had "a recorded history of passive homosexual involvement and current homosexual behavior and a necessity for strict segregation."[29] These men continue to be designated as "Category 'B' Effeminate Homosexuals."

Even with the new classification system, the CDC maintains procedures for the placement of different types of inmates for each of the penal institutions throughout the state. The flamboyant homosexuals requiring special counseling and the transsexuals, for example, are housed in one particular institution.

Correspondence with one of the top administrators of this other facility revealed that there has not been any appreciable change in the attitudes or rules regarding homosexuals, although he added, "The increasing laxity of today's society's view toward these individuals was reflected by staff's increasing acceptance and tolerance."

This administrator also added that in recent years they had encountered a new phenomenon—a group of transsexuals who had undergone some medical treatment outside prison (and therefore had developed breasts) but who had not completed the surgical alterations and were thus considered technically to be males. The policy in dealing with these people was not to encourage further treatment (i.e., sex-change operation) nor to discourage the progress that had been made (i.e., by not withholding hormone therapy). Thus, according to this prison official, they were keeping these persons at the status quo level and it was then up to them to receive further treatment and/or operations upon parole to the community.

No transsexuals were housed in the prison we studied. As our data on the homosexuals showed, there were several effeminate homosexuals (mostly black) who indicated a preference for being female, although they contended they were happy with their present sexual identities.

Even though the *Classification Manual* in the past has set forth elaborate placement procedures and criteria, *in actuality* many different types of inmates are mixed together and assigned to institutions which are not specifically equipped to handle them. It appears that *racial balance* and ethnic placement are prime criteria for the classification committee in placing an individual in a specific institution, and even in the assigned job within each institution. Throughout the CDC there is a strict policy of maintaining racial balance so as to discourage gang-related hostility. These concerns, combined with the issue of bed-space availability in these overcrowded institutions, appear to take precedence over the placement needs and best interests of those inmates most likely to be vulnerable to sexual assault. Sometimes, too, particular penal institutions have quotas with respect to the numbers of certain types of homosexuals they can adequately house. (In 1979 the established quota for effeminate homosexuals was sixty for the prison under study.) It is for these reasons that many passive homosexuals and heterosexual kids get sent to hard-core institutions; likewise, many of the aggressive jockers are assigned to prisons designated for the vulnerable inmates.

The placement procedures employed by the CDC that send homosexuals to these more difficult institutions were open to criticism by many inmates in our study. It appears, as the following account indicates, that not all homosexuals who fit the criteria of being passive, overt, and even feminine, are automatically assigned to the two prisons that are designated and equipped to handle them. Many homosexuals are apparently sent to the more violence-prone institutions even when they voice their concern about such potential placement. One prison homosexual named "Jim" shared this account with us:

### "Jim"

"I'll describe for you the classification and placement determination procedure, using my case as an example. The CDC has two reception centers—one at Chino, serving the southern counties, and one at Vacaville, serving the northern counties. Once an inmate is sentenced to state prison, the county sheriff transports him to one of these two reception centers for processing. Upon arrival at the reception center the inmates receive extensive psychological testing, background investigation, and medical examinations. Each man is then assigned a counselor who compiles an extensive "Cumulative Case Summary" and meets with the inmate to discuss his future while in prison. This first meeting is quite brief, about three to five minutes. Approximately two weeks later the man meets with the counselor for the final time, again briefly, and is told the counselor's recommendation regarding placement and programming. [Programming refers to recommendation as to type of work, vocational trade, or schooling.]

During my stay at the guidance and reception center, I had got the rundown on most of the various institutions from the other inmates, most of whom were two- or three-termers. When I went to see my counselor for the first time, I stressed that I was a first-termer, that I was passive, that I had no history of violence, and that I was a homosexual and did not want to be placed in a hard-core joint. I requested this prison [under study] as my first choice and California Men's Colony as my second choice. When I went in for my second interview with the counselor he informed me that he was recommending that I be sent to San Quentin. I had been sent to prison for burglary and did not feel that I deserved such a "stiff" placement. Also, I again stressed that because I was a homosexual I felt that I would be subjected to a great deal of pressure and abuse, but my counselor could have cared less.

When I returned to my housing unit I discussed this with some of the older joint-wise cons who I worked with, and they all told me that for my own good, I definitely did not want to get sent to San Quentin. They suggested that I file a "602" [inmate appeal form] on the counselor's recommendation. The CDC has a policy whereby an inmate may appeal any staff decision in several stages up a successive chain of authority, to Sacramento, and even ultimately to the courts. However, about 90% of the time it is wasted energy. Anyway, I did appeal the decision. According to CDC regulations, you must have a hearing on your first-level appeal within ten days; however, I never received any hearing.

The classification procedure goes like this. The counselor makes his recommendation; it then goes to his supervisor to concur or disapprove it. Then once every week a classification staff representative from Sacramento comes to the guidance center and reviews all placement recommendations, and he has final say. In my case, both my counselor and his supervisor recommended San Quentin; however, when the CSR reviewed my file he overrode their decision and sent me to this prison, thank God.

I was lucky. There are many who are not—especially passive youngsters. The counselor assigned to me told me that San Quentin would "make a man out of me." This type of thinking is prevalent throughout the system. The cruelty toward homosexuals, the rapes, and all the brutality is seen by the officials as "just the way it is in prison," and "if you don't want to be involved, you shouldn't get sent to prison in the first place."

Such insensitivity by the prison officials in sending these vulnerable inmates to the hard-core institutions where there is a greater likelihood for sexual victimization and exploitation to take place is not the only problem inherent in the prison system. Other concerns have to do with staffing and personnel matters.

## STAFFING AND PERSONNEL POLICY

According to the associate superintendent of the prison we studied, since the mid-1970s the CDC has moved away from hiring ex-military-type personnel (the so-called "stiff upper lip" type, in the words of this administrator), and has hired personnel who exhibit a mixture of authoritarian *and* humanitarian traits. (The policy deputy director of the CDC concurred with this statement and informed us that their "ideal" personnel type was the "kindly authoritarian.")

The administration now considers of prime importance the officer's ability to express his feelings and concern toward those inmates whom he respects. According to the associate superintendent, the administration does not wish to cultivate an adversary climate between prison personnel and the inmates. Since these convicts are in this medium-security prison for rehabilitative purposes, and since they are usually short-termers, it is the administration's philosophy that the climate in prison should be as conducive to positive staff and inmate relations as can be developed within the confines of the prison situation.

To this end the prison established a joint task force in 1980 to work on the ways to improve staff and inmate relations. According to the eight-person committee's final report, there were many areas that warranted improvement. The committee recommended that training workshops in the field of communication be developed so that each side could interact more responsibly; that the inmates have input into the In-Service Training of the new correctional officers; that the staff in particular learn to act in a professional manner and not to respond inappropriately to inmate behavior; and that mandatory, weekly meetings comprised of no more than twenty inmates to one staff member be initiated so that all participants are able to air their opinions without fear of reprisal.[30]

The prison administration, we feel, is to be commended for taking the initiative in forming this committee, and it is our hope that the task force's recommendations will be adopted as prison policy and be implemented accordingly. Increasing the opportunities for dialogue would not only improve the rapport between inmates and staff, but should also lessen the exploitive nature of prison sexuality among the inmates themselves—our primary concern. As a recent study on prison victimization found, "The way in which correctional officers treat prisoners may be a significant factor in the level of prisoner violence that occurs in an institution."[31]

## DEVELOPMENT OF PROGRAMS FOR INMATES

As we have shown, the prison situation creates an atmosphere which encourages the inmates—regardless of sexual orientation—to play games of dominance, conquest, manipulation, and exploitation. The continued presence of this pattern, we feel, though part of human nature, is counterproductive to the goal of rehabilitation that the prison is mandated to achieve. As the prison joint task force for improved inmate and staff relations found, the benefits of improved communication would be fewer arguments, reduced disciplinary incidents, "a better all-around 'air' about the whole institution," and "improved attitudes interpersonally that can be utilized out on the streets" by staff and parolees alike. By improving communications, and thereby lessening the tension in prison which leads to sexual victimization and manipulation, the prison would achieve its goal of improving the success rate of the inmates once they are released from custody.[32]

It is our contention that the goal of prison rehabilitation should be to try to improve the quality of human interaction and individual self-worth. In this regard, we are not specifically critical of sexual behavior in prison per se. Sexual activity in prison is a fact of life. To limit or curtail such behavior in prison is a virtual impossibility since it would require nearly total lockdown and individual, around-the-clock surveillance. The administration can, however, restrict the exploitive nature of this activity by separating the aggressors from the potential victims, and by continuing to work to improve the communications skills and interpersonal relations of both inmates and staff.

To reiterate, our criticism is of the exploitive aspects of prison sexuality. We do not feel that inmates should be allowed (or encouraged) to be exploitive, nor do we feel inmates should be placed in an environment that knowingly allows them to be exploited. We support programs and policies that would assist all inmates—regardless of their sexual orientation—to come to grips with their personal lives, to learn to become productive and law-abiding citizens, and to be rehabilitated to the degree that when they are subsequently released back into society, they are better equipped to function in a nonmaladaptive way. Unfortunately, the penal system is *not* accomplishing these formidable tasks. At best it is enhancing opportunities for continued maladaptive behavior. The exploitive nature of prison sexuality is a clear indication of the prison's failure to achieve its goals. It appears that a term in state prison merely exacerbates the criminal tendencies of many of its inmates.

These observations and conclusions are also shared to a certain degree by the CDC. According to the policy deputy director, the counseling programs do not always receive the highest priority in prison. Strapped by limited financial resources and severe overcrowding, prison authorities are not always able to isolate particular groups such as those who have been sexually victimized and to provide them with counseling. It appears that the current economic and social climate is not conducive to providing improved assistance programs. In the words of the administrator, the prison authorities have little "maneuvering room" and, with few options, the "short-range picture is very gloomy." Furthermore, prison wardens do not get fired if their counseling programs do not work. Instead, they get fired if they lose control of the prison as a result of racial disturbances or inmate insurrections which get media attention. Since these matters are more critical to the prison officials, the concerns of the victims of sexual assault become low-priority items.

Even with this "gloomy" picture, we feel that efforts to assist the homosexuals (and punks) in prison in developing a positive self-image are beneficial to society at large as they better prepare these individuals to become self-actualizing and responsible citizens. While certain individuals or groups in the public sector may not approve of homosexual behavior per se, and may personally dislike homosexuals, we feel that the general public would welcome any effort or program which would allow these people to reach their full potential as responsible, contributing members to society. Thus even those who condemn homosexuality can still see merit in supporting programs which assist prison homosexuals to develop a more positive self-image, if for no other reason than that such a change would lessen recidivism and antisocial behavior. As other studies have found, we are suggesting that a causal relationship exists between a positive self-identity for gay people and the lessening of their disruptive social behavior.[33]

To this end, one of the efforts to rehabilitate homosexuals and to assist them in coping with their sexual identities and/or sexual victimization has been the introduction of specific programs for these men, most particularly in those prisons which house many "known" homosexuals. Such programs, as we shall now discuss, were beginning to be implemented in the prison under study.

## GAY ACTIVITIES AND ORGANIZATIONS IN PRISON

Outside of a few select individuals, a positively affirmed gay identity has not entered this prison environment, and definitely not as any type of organized movement or support group. One reason for this is that very few self-aware and educated individuals (regardless of their sexual orientation) are sent to prison. The notion that it is only the poor and disenfranchised members of our society who are sent to prison is generally true. Almost anyone with sufficient money to hire a private attorney, or who comes from a middle-class, financially productive background will not be sent to prison unless his crime was extremely violent or it was his third or fourth offense.

It appears that both the prison placement policy (i.e., sending the effeminate homosexuals to this prison) and the type of identity these homosexuals bring with them to prison (i.e., a feminine identity for the most part) create a prison norm for homosexuals that *matches* the expectation of the convict prison sexual code. In this respect a modern gay identity (i.e., autonomous, masculine, sensitive) is definitely out of place in this environment.

Because of this pattern there has been no attempt by the homosexual community within this prison to question their status. Basically, homosexuals in prison are unorganized and passive; they are in no way dynamic or goal directed. They merely react to the pressures and circumstances imposed upon them by the overpowering convict social system.

Furthermore, no homosexual was sent to this prison because of gay political activism or civil disobedience related to the gay movement. In fact, compared to other social movements such as the black movement and the student activism of the 1960s, the gay movement has not generated the tactics of street violence or subterfuge. In this respect, few if any homosexuals are incarcerated for behavior related to gay activism.

We raise this remote issue because several inmates interviewed in our prison study were incarcerated for terrorist activities stemming from the period of civil disobedience of the past two decades. These inmates were not homosexual, but their treatment in prison by both staff and the other inmates was distinct. These inmates, who had received a great deal of pretrial publicity, informed us that they had been pressured by other inmates not in a sexual context but in a political context. They were looked up to by the other inmates who, in the case of the racial gangs, wanted them to join up and become their spokesmen.

The only organization for homosexuals that is active in this prison is the *Metropolitan Community Church* (MCC). However, it basically functions as little more than a social group in the guise of religion. The services are conducted on a weekly basis (on Monday nights) by a lesbian minister who delivers mildly inspirational sermonettes that are lacking in any real consciousness-raising content or practical relevance to the homosexual inmate. A typical service begins with a call to worship and prayer, followed by a twenty-minute sermonette and a concluding prayer. Communion is periodically served to those wishing to take part. Over the past five years the membership has grown to 150 inmates, according to the associate superintendent, although only fifty or so regularly show up at the meetings.

The prison administration supports this program as it sees these church sessions as a means of building "inward strength" among the homosexuals. At one time, however, the meetings were being interrupted by the intimidating presence of black jockers who were using the meetings, in the words of the supervisor, to "spot future sexual partners and conquests."

At the conclusion of the formal portion of the service the participants are allowed to gossip and socialize for approximately half an hour. The atmosphere is casual and relaxed. One gets the impression that the socializing is of more interest and importance to the participants than the religious service.

The MCC started conducting services in this prison in 1976 after some inmates here filed a class-action suit in which the California Supreme Court ultimately decided to allow the MCC access to the inmate population. The services are conducted in the visiting room and are not supervised by the "custody" personnel. The associate superintendent periodically attends the meetings to show support for the group's activities.

Outside of this weekly service, which does provide homosexual inmates from different quads an opportunity to get together and visit, homosexuals in this prison setting tend not to form formal cliques or friendship groups. Within each quad most of the outfront homosexuals know each other, and there is a tendency among them to hang out together on a casual basis. The black queens in particular get together to gossip, socialize, and perhaps do each other's hair. Most of the interquad gossip is passed about among the queens.

Even with these MCC services, in terms of the *gay identity formation model* formulated by Vivienne C. Cass,[34] neither the positive identities of "pride" nor "synthesis" (the last two stages of the six-stage model) was present within the prison. That is, there was an absence of homosexual men who take pride in their gay identity and who have organized together in terms of a gay movement. While many "sissies" in prison indicated they were content with their sexual identity, the fact that very few self-actualized gay men were in prison (or were open about their homosexuality) has meant that gay identity—both individually and collectively—has remained at less advanced stages of development (according to the Cass model) compared to the gay subculture that is developing external to the prison environment.

The "gay liberation" message, and gay awareness issues as presented in the media do get through and are heard in prison. Gay publications, including newspapers and magazines, are now allowed in prison although access is regulated by each prison system. The inmate norms and scripts are nonetheless deeply ingrained and slow to change. There is definitely a cultural lag in prison in that changes in attitudes are occurring outside prison much faster than they are inside.

Obviously, gay consciousness-raising groups or support groups in prison, courses which include information on the gay experience for the staff and inmates, sensitizing sessions dealing with topics such as sexuality, and a greater access by homosexual prisoners to support groups on the outside would improve the homosexual's feelings of self-worth within the prison walls. Such endeavors would be effective vehicles for change; however, they would never be able to develop and function in any but the most lenient of the prison environments.

The first gay organization to be formed inside prison to address the concerns of homosexual inmates is the *Sexual Minority Prisoners' Caucus* (SMPC) of the Washington State Reformatory. This prisoner's organization serves as a model for gay organizations attempting to get started in other prisons across the country. The SMPC publishes a monthly newsletter as well as a brochure explaining their program.

According to their brochure, the caucus was organized in 1979 to "combat sexual abuse and assault of gay prisoners." Although not officially sanctioned by the prison authorities, the SMPC has received endorsements from the local press and external organizations. Caucus members meet the "weekly 'chain' of new prisoners" and provide assistance and support "to those men most likely to be raped, sold, pimped, and preyed upon in the sexual meat market condoned by the administration." The members try to provide "safe houses" for the new prisoners, which they define as "cells in which people can live temporarily protected from constant threats of sexual violence and abuse while they develop their own support and protection networks." The SMPC also sponsors educational forums and seminars "designed to raise consciousness levels of straight prisoners, prison staff, and outsiders," and meets with a community board of advisors which acts as a support group and which assists paroled inmates in finding employment.[35]

In correspondence with officers of the SMPC in February 1981, we were informed that although the caucus had not received official recognition, they were allowed to hold meetings with outside guests and order office supplies from the state. The caucus also raises money to cover operating expenses by selling craft items in the Visitor's Store, selling club T-shirts, receiving donations, and selling subscriptions to their newsletter. The organization's long-range goals are to "obtain a gay halfway house, to provide court services for gays who are first offenders, and to recommend deterrents to prison for gay first-offenders."[36]

Outside of the role that the MCC plays in providing religious services for homosexual inmates and the activities of the SMPC in the Washington prison, no other known gay organization has developed within the prison environment. In the prison we studied only the MCC is in operation, although many of the programs and reforms that the SMPC has developed are similar to programs that the homosexuals in our prison sample strongly recommended and endorsed. There are, however, some organizations external to the prison setting that are actively involved in prison reform.

## THE ROLE OF THE NONPRISON COMMUNITY

Interest in the situation in America's prisons has dramatically increased in recent years even though a stronger "law and order" sentiment is sending criminals to prison on a more frequent basis and for longer sentences. Concern about the sexual exploitation of homosexuals and "kids" has long been expressed by both the straight and gay communities. Recent publications about prison sexual violence have assisted in drawing the public's attention to this common pattern. Prison rape and sexual assault have been the theme of numerous motion pictures (Brubaker, Penitentiary, Straight Time) and television shows ("60 Minutes," "Scared Straight") over the past few years. Another recent movie (Stir Crazy) depicted a "black prison sissy" in a favorable light. Press accounts of prison uprisings and disturbances have also shed light on the (mis)treatment of homosexuals and punks. In the coverage of the New Mexico prison riot in 1980, for example, the press accurately noted that because many homosexuals were housed in protective custody where the "snitches" were also housed, the homosexuals were indiscriminately attacked and even murdered by other convicts when they went on their rampage. Furthermore, politicans, editorial writers, political action groups, and concerned citizens have all recently voiced their opinions about prison conditions in America. Some judges, in fact, have refused to invoke prison sentences on first-offenders since a state prison term, in their judgment (and in ours), would "do more harm than good."

Even with these concerns, however, the increasingly conservative drift of American society in this decade suggests an attitude which is likely to see stiffer sentencing. The general public has come to view incarceration, even with its threat of sexual violence, as the necessary means to combat crime, stem violence, and protect the citizenry of the nation. The electorate has voted into office those politicans who campaign on strong "law and order" platforms ("Use a Gun, Go to Jail" was the campaign slogan of the recently elected attorney-general for the State of California). With prisons already overcrowded and a sagging economy unable—or a public unwilling—to allocate funds for new prison construction and staffing, the conditions in our nation's prisons will continue to deteriorate. If anything, as numerous studies have shown, overcrowding leads to increased inmate tensions, hostility, and sexual exploitation.[37] Such trends likewise will have an impact on rehabilitation efforts since needed services and programs for the inmates will become severely reduced and impaired.

Although reformers in the past have successfully lobbied for the abolition of arrangements that placed some

prisoners in control of others, for limiting inmate popula-
tions to prevent overcrowding, and for improved medical,
educational, occupational, and mental health services, the
public's increased fears about crime and its attitude toward
the role of prisons in confining and punishing offenders
have created a social climate that is basically *nonsupportive*
of prison reform. Judging from the political climate of
today, there appears to be minimal support from the public
to change the system.

Even in this atmosphere, however, some reform
efforts and innovative programs to assist the prison
inmates, and particularly those men who are victims of
sexual exploitation, continue to persist. The pioneering
work of the Metropolitan Community Church has led to
an expansion of church services for homosexuals in prisons
in many states. Further, the MCC has developed programs
which provide homosexual inmates with penpals, visitations where location and regulations permit, information
about correspondence studies through local schools, and
parole assistance in helping the homosexuals find housing,
food, and employment upon their release.

As stated in our opening chapter, the *National Gay Task
Force*, an organization formed to coordinate nationwide
efforts to improve the lives and social conditions of gay
men and lesbians in society, has marked the improvement
of conditions for homosexuals in prison as one of their
priority agenda items for the 1980s. To assist in this formidable effort, many other independent gay and nongay
organizations across the country are developing programs
to help remedy the situation in our nation's prisons.

The efforts of the National Gay Task Force (NGTF)
with regard to prison reform have concentrated on litigation and negotiation. Since 1978 representatives of the
"prison project" of the NGTF have met on a regular basis
with the director of the Federal Bureau of Prisons. The

results of these consultations have brought about such changes as the inclusion of the national gay community in the sensitivity-training sessions of many of the federal prisons, the appointment of a staff member of the bureau to deal directly with complaints from gay inmates, and the decision to provide the NGTF with "full details of Bureau guidelines on classification of prisoners, parole recommendations and the like; and statistics on segregation of prisoners and related matters such as denial of educational and recreational facilities."[38]

A further tangible result of these joint meetings is the policy to prohibit the use of such misleading terms as "homosexual rape" and "homosexual assault" when discussing prison sexual violence. As our study concluded, it is the aggressive heterosexual and bisexual jockers who are the instigators of sexual violence. Accordingly, the Federal Bureau of Prisons announced in 1978 that "Through the use of such terms, the public is led to believe that these assaults are committed by persons who are homosexual. While homosexuals are frequently the victims, the vast majority of rapes and assaults are committed by persons who are not homosexual."[39]

Other efforts by the National Gay Task Force have involved the development of a policy with regard to the distribution to prisoners of certain gay-oriented publications. The new Federal Bureau of Prisons policy stipulates that gay publications of a news or informational nature, gay literary publications, and publications of gay religious groups should be admitted to prison. A local warden may exclude sexually explicit material, although material that has scholarly, general, social, or literary value may not be excluded. The NGTF considered this decision to be especially welcome since it "will contribute to the rehabilitation process by providing gay prisoners with news and information that is fundamental to their morale, sense of identity and hope for the future."[40]

Another organization which has worked for prison reform is the *American Civil Liberties Union* (ACLU). This organization has long had a National Prison Project which works to humanize the prison experience; it is concerned with the civil rights deprivations of all prisoners. In 1980 the National Gay Rights Project of the ACLU established a Gay Prisoners Committee to document incidents of discrimination or abuse suffered by lesbian and gay prisoners at the hands of police, the courts, jail or prison personnel, or other prisoners. The committee further stated that "By using litigation, lobbying, and media techniques developed by ACLU's National Prisoners' Rights Project, the new committee will bring the resources of ACLU's state affiliates and volunteer attorneys to bear on the problem."[41]

The Southern California chapter of the ACLU is currently considering handling litigation of charges by a prison inmate who has alleged that jail personnel subjected him to harsh treatment by forcing him to wear a pink armband which made it easier for other prisoners in county jail to identify him as a homosexual and "hit upon him."

Another organization involved with prison reform is the *National Moratorium on Prison Construction* (NMPC), founded in 1975 by the Unitarian-Universalist Service Committee. Their primary focus is to develop alternatives to incarceration as well as to monitor the construction of new penal facilities. Their list of "alternatives" to jail and prison include the development of "Release on Recognizance" programs; third-party supervised-release programs; and probation, community service programs, and residential community-based centers for non-hard-core prisoners.

Besides these political, social, and humanitarian organizations, efforts on behalf of prison reform have been implemented by several gay newspapers and magazines. Many national and local gay periodicals are specifically involved with providing their readers with articles, programs such as penpals, and services directed toward the homosexual prisoner. The *Gaycon Press Newsletter*, for example, published in San Francisco, provides information on the status of various gay inmates and gay organizations that are beginning to develop in prison. It also lists the publications that are available free to gay prisoners. These include: *The Advocate* (San Francisco, California), *Fag Rag* (Cambridge, Massachusetts), *Cellmate* (MCC newsletter, Los Angeles), the *San Francisco Crusader*, the *Gay Community News* (Boston), *RFD* (Bakersville, North Carolina), and the *Guardian* (New York City). Many of these newspapers carry a "Prisoner's Page" *(Gay Community News)* or a "Brothers Behind Bars" section *(RFD)* which are mostly contact letters from prisoners and occasional news blurbs. Most of these newspapers are free to the inmates who request (and are permitted to receive) them.

Coverage sympathetic to the victims of prison sexual assault has also been found in the nongay press as well. An excellent personal account of life in prison written by an inmate which focuses on the inhumanity of the prison experience was published in 1980 by the *New York Review*.[42] Other accounts of prison life for homosexuals have been published in the gay monthly literary magazine, *Christopher Street*.[43] Recent controversy over a paroled convict who allegedly stabbed a restaurant employee in New York City has generated public interest in reading his account (in the form of letters) of prison life in his book *In the Belly of the Beast*.[44]

Besides the organizations previously mentioned, there are several other regional and national organizations involved with prison reform which directly or indirectly affect the submissive heterosexual youngsters and the homosexuals. These organizations include: The National Prison Reform Advisory Board (PRAB) of the Religious Council of America; the Prison Art Project, which promotes artistic expression by providing materials and instructions in painting and photography for inmates; Ending Unnecessary Imprisonment in New York State, Task Force for a Safer Society of the New York State Council of Churches; the Fortune Society; the New York Gay Prisoner Support Committee; and the Committee to Abolish Prison Slavery.

Besides these endeavors, many local gay and lesbian organizations have received permission to provide entertainment and programs inside prison. The Gay and Lesbian Chorus of Los Angeles, for example, in 1980 gave a free concert in one of California's prisons.

### CONCLUSIONS AND QUESTIONS OF CONCERN

The goal articulated by the National Gay Task Force—to rectify prison conditions that deny gay prisoners equal opportunity for recreation, education, and parole, that prevent them from reading gay newspapers and from seeing gay ministers, and that allow for the continued assault and rape of gay prisoners—is beginning to be met in some prisons. Many areas of concern expressed by the NGTF were *not* critical to the prison we have studied, and the situation appears to be improving in certain prisons nationwide. The larger issues of sexual assault, and the continued lack of programs for heterosexual youngsters who are sexually victimized, however, remain relevant concerns for all prisons, including the one under study.

Sexual exploitation in prison is an actuality. Most such assaults are carried out by persons who anywhere else would be involved in heterosexual acts, and who would be, by all standards, heterosexual. The targets of the assaults tend to be the young, the good-looking heterosexual, and the known homosexual. These are persons the assaulter tends to treat like females.

Prison for the homosexual prisoner—as it is for most prisoners—is a dangerous, deadly, and dehumanizing place. The homosexuals and heterosexual youngsters in prison live in fear of being exploited. They are abused by other inmates and in some prisons even by those persons working in the system. Rehabilitation of prisoners in such an environment is negligible. Some prison authorities on the other hand contend that the perpetuation of this situation acts as a deterrent, since individuals contemplating committing serious crimes might have second thoughts if they knew that they would be incarcerated under such conditions.

We feel, however, that such prison environments should not be encouraged to exist. By maintaining these social patterns the prisons serve as breeding grounds for maladaptive behavior. But how can the situation be remedied? What can be done to reduce the sexual victimization of males in our nation's prisons? Is this situation inevitable among the "criminal element" in society? Does the cultural adaptation that emerges in prison have to be one which allows aggressive and dominant inmates to use sexuality as the basic means of control?

Throughout this study we have presented suggestions made by our prison informants. They felt that those inmates most vulnerable to sexual assault should be housed separately on one floor of the prison, should receive counseling and assistance by staff members sensitive to their problems, and should not be placed in an environment which freely lets the aggressive jockers maintain control. Further, they felt that special attention should be given to the "kids" who had been sexually victimized, and they supported proposed programs aimed at improving the communication between staff and inmates.

Our study has also raised many questions. After analyzing our data, we approached the prison administration

with some of the following questions pertaining to the
results and findings. Very few of these issues were satisfactorily answered by the associate superintendent. Some
of the study's findings, the administrator admitted, were
surprising, and some questions we raised pertained to
issues that the prison officials had not been asked to consider before. Among these were:

- Our study found that 9% of the heterosexual men
  had been sexually assaulted since coming to this
  prison. What is the prison doing about this, and
  what should it be doing about it?
- Our study found that 41% of the homosexuals had
  been pressured into sex. What is the prison doing
  about this, and what should the prison be doing
  about it?
- The whole issue of homosexual behavior and sex
  between consenting adults is very complex, particularly in states like California where the laws concerning such activity are more lenient than they are
  in other parts of the country. How does this affect
  the prison setting and inmate behavior?
- Will the current conservative climate of the 1980s
  affect any of the more liberal trends of the preceding
  decade with regard to homosexual behavior and
  programs for homosexuals in prison? In other
  words, does the political climate in both the state
  and the nation have much of an impact on prison
  policy with regard to sexuality?
- What special assistance can be given to the punks
  who refuse to identify themselves to prison authorities because of the stigma of being labeled a
  "snitch?" (This is of particular concern since a recent
  study has shown that they are likely to be predis-
  posed to violence as a result of their own sexual vic-

timization while incarcerated.) How can the prison assist the victim from becoming the potential victimizer?

- As society has turned toward a more law-and-order approach in sentencing, the prisons have filled with much younger men who often in the past would likely not have been incarcerated in adult prisons. How will this new pattern affect sexual aggression, since it is these younger men who are likely to become either the victims or the perpetrators? What is the prison doing to prepare for this probable increase in sexual violence?

- The men in this medium-security prison are likely to be paroled at some future date. How has their prison experience shaped their sexual selves in light of the fact that so many self-defined heterosexual and bisexual inmates reported sexual activity?

- Since this particular prison is one of several which receives the majority of homosexuals who are incarcerated in the California penal system, what will be (and should be) the prison's role with respect to them?

- Some of our findings indicated, for example, that homosexuals have been sent to prison for less serious offenses, and are viewed by staff personnel as causing fewer disciplinary problems. If this is the case, is this the type of penal institution where they should have been sent? Are there special programs, activities, and support systems for these men? Should there be?

- Are there programs that can be introduced into this prison which would benefit those men most vulnerable to prison sexual exploitation in which cost is *not* a factor?

- What about such practices as conjugal visits for

homosexuals? Should sexual pairing for two homosexuals (as opposed to a jocker and a sissy) be
encouraged in prison even though the convict code
is threatened by that?

- Our study shows that heterosexual inmates who
were sexually active in prison were just as likely to
be married as to be single, separated, or divorced.
Furthermore, those heterosexuals who were married
and received conjugal visits were slightly more sexually active in prison than those heterosexuals who
were married whose wives did not visit them. Are
these findings a surprise?

- There appear to be enormous ethnic differences
with respect to sexual behavior and attitudes toward
sexuality. How can the prison system work to sen-
sitize both convicts and staff personnel to these significant racial, ethnic, and cultural differences?

- The Mexican-American homosexuals reported great-
est dissatisfaction with their treatment by prison
personnel. What are the reasons for this finding?

- The black effeminate homosexuals reported both
better and more frequent sex in prison compared to
their sexual experiences outside of prison. What distinctive role do these men play in prison and how
do the prison authorities view these men?

- On the whole, the prison staff is viewed by many
homosexuals (35%) as being sensitive, and in fact
our interviews with correctional officers indicate a
quite supportive concern. Is this finding surprising?
What specific training are the officers given with
respect to prison sexuality and the issue of homosexuality and the gay lifestyle?

- Have "open" gay men and lesbians been hired to
work in this prison? Is this an appropriate consideration since many homosexuals are housed here?

Would homosexual personnel have difficulty with other staff members? Would there be any benefits to the institution and its programs if "open" lesbians and gay men were hired?

- The gay movement both on a national level and locally within the state of California is concerned about the fate of homosexuals and vulnerable heterosexual youngsters in prison. How does this lobbyist and political group affect this prison, if at all?
- What impact do studies such as this one have on prison policy? What kind of impact should they have?

As we stated, very few of these questions were answered to our satisfaction. Nor do we have ready solutions. We do feel, however, that these important questions and issues should be raised for public debate.

If our study has been of any benefit, it has shown the dynamics of sexual behavior and sexual exploitation as they exist in a medium-security prison—a prison which has begun to deal realistically with certain critical issues. We encourage these and other efforts. As things now stand, however, life for a number of men behind bars remains a criminal act itself.

# Notes

1. "Media Guide to Gay Issues," National Gay Task Force, 80 Fifth Ave., Suite 1601, New York, NY 10011.
2. David A. Shore, *Sex-Related Issues in Correctional Facilities: A Classified Bibliography* (Chicago: The Playboy Foundation, 1981). This up-to-date bibliography lists 203 references in several key areas: men, women, juveniles, corrections, conjugal visits, relationships, and legal issues.
3. Center for Research and Education in Sexuality (C.E.R.E.S.), John P. DeCecco, director, San Francisco State University, San Francisco, CA 94132.
4. Rose Giallombardo, *Society of Women: A Study of a Women's Prison* (New York: John Wiley & Sons, 1966).
5. John H. Gagnon, *Human Sexualities* (Glenville, Ill.: Scott, Foresman & Company, 1977).
6. Giallombardo, *Society of Women.*
7. Laud Humphreys, *Tearoom Trade: Impersonal Sex in Public Places* (Hawthorne, NY: Aldine, 1975).
8. Charles W. Thomas, "Theoretical Perspectives on Prisonization: A Comparison of the Importation and Deprivation Models," *Journal of Criminal Law and Criminology* 68, no. 1 (1977): 135–145.
9. Ibid.
10. Leo Carroll, *Hacks, Blacks, and Cons: Race Relations in a Maximum Security Prison* (Lexington, Mass.: D. C. Heath, 1974).
11. Theodore H. Davidson, *Chicano Prisoners: The Key to San Quentin* (New York: Holt, Rinehart & Winston, 1974).
12. Anthony M. Scacco, *Rape in Prison* (Springfield, Ill.: Charles C Thomas, 1975).

233

13. Alfred Kinsey, Wardell B. Pomeroy, and Clyde E. Martin, *Sexual Behavior in the Human Male* (Philadelphia: W. B. Saunders, 1948).

14. Brian Miller and Laud Humphreys, "Lifestyles and Violence: Homosexual Victims of Assault and Murder," *Qualitative Sociology* 3 (Fall 1980): 169–185.

15. A. Nicholas Groth with H. Jean Birnbaum, *Men Who Rape: The Psychology of the Offender* (New York: Plenum Press, 1979).

16. Barry M. Dank, "Coming Out in the Gay World," *Psychiatry* 34 (May 1971): 180–97.

17. Alan P. Bell and Martin S. Weinberg, *Homosexualities: A Study of Diversity Among Men & Women* (New York: Simon & Schuster, 1978).

18. Laud Humphreys, "Exodus and Identity: The Emerging Gay Culture," in Martin Levine, ed., *Gay Men: The Sociology of Male Homosexuality* (New York: Harper & Row, 1979), pp. 134–47.

19. Charles Silverstein, *Man to Man: Gay Couples in America* (New York: William Morrow & Company, 1981).

20. Gregory K. Lehne, "Homophobia Among Men," in D. David and R. Brannon, eds., *The Forty-Nine Percent Majority: The Male Sex Role* (New York: Addison-Wesley, 1976).

21. Stephen F. Morin and Ellen M. Garfinkle, "Male Homophobia," *Journal of Social Issues* 34 (Winter 1978): 29–47.

22. E. E. Levitt and A. D. Klassen, "Public Attitudes Toward Homosexuality," *Journal of Homosexuality* 1 (1974): 29–43.

23. Monika B. Reed and Francis D. Glamser, "Aging in a Total Institution: The Case of Older Prisoners," *The Gerontologist* 19 (1979): 354–60.

24. United States National Criminal Justice Information and Statistics Service, *Sourcebook of Criminal Justice Statistics* (Washington, D.C.: U.S. Government Printing Office, 1977).

25. State of California Department of Corrections, Health and Welfare Agency, "Characteristics of Felon Population in California State Prisons By Institution," June 30, 1979, 1980.

26. John Irwin and Donald R. Cressey, "Thieves, Convicts and the Inmate Culture," *Social Problems* 10 (1962): 142–53.

27. Louis Dwight, "The Sin of Sodom is the Vice of Prisoners . . ." in Jonathan Katz, *Gay American History: Lesbians and Gay Men in the U.S.A.* (New York: Avon Books, 1978), pp. 42–45.

28. State of California Department of Corrections, "Operational Implementation of the Classification System," Administrative Bulletin no. 80/61, Dec. 16, 1980; and id., "Institutional Security Levels," Dec. 9, 1981.

29. Id., *Classification Manual*, Chapter 2200, "Treatment Categories," Sept. 1, 1978.

30. Id., "Departmental Task Force on Staff/Inmate Relations," Administrative Bulletin no. 80/28, Sept. 19, 1980.

31. Lee H. Bowker, *Prison Victimization* (New York: Elsevier Press, 1980), p. 176.

32. CDC, "Departmental Task Force on Staff/Inmate Relations."

33. Vivienne C. Cass, "Homosexual Identity Formation: A theoretical Model," *Journal of Homosexuality* 4 (Spring 1979): 219–35.

34. Ibid.

35. "Sexual Minority Prisoners' Caucus," Washington State Reformatory, P.O. Box 777, Monroe, WA 98272.

36. Ibid.

37. John Irwin, *Prisons in Turmoil* (Boston: Little, Brown and Company, 1980).

38. "NGTF Holds Meeting with Bureau of Prisons: Carlson Agrees to Staff 'Sensitivity Training,'" National Gay Task Force press release, March 22, 1978 (NGTF, 80 Fifth Ave., New York, NY 10011).

39. "Prison Rapes No Longer Labeled 'Homosexual Assault,'" National Gay Task Force press release, April 19, 1978.

40. "Federal Prisons to Admit Gay Publications," National Gay Task Force press release, Oct. 22, 1980.

41. "Project Description," National Prison Project, American Civil Liberties Union Foundation (132 W. 43 St., New York, NY 10036).

42. Jack H. Abbott, "In Prison," *New York Review*, June 26, 1980.

43. Ted Nicholas, "Pooftahs in English Prisons," *Christopher Street*, June 1977, pp. 31–34.

44. Jack H. Abbott, *In the Belly of the Beast: Letters from Prison* (New York: Random House, 1981).

# Appendix A

## Questionaires

This is an anonymous survey. Please answer each question by filling in the blank or circling the appropriate response. *Do not* write your name on this paper.

1. What is your age? _____
2. What is your race? _____ Black _____ Caucasian _____ Hispanic _____ Other
3. What crime were you sent to prison for? _____
4. How long a sentence did you receive? _____
5. What is the date of your I.D. card? _____
6. Is this your: _____ First _____ Second _____ Third prison term?
7. Are you: _____ Single _____ Married _____ Separated _____ Divorced
8. If married, how often do you get conjugal visits? _____

*Since coming to prison this term:*

9. How often do you masturbate? _____

10. I have often had sexual experiences with approximately _____ different inmates.

11. I have been orally copulated approximately _____ times.

12. I have performed anal intercourse on other inmates approximately _____ times.

13. I have orally copulated other inmates approximately _____ times.

14. I have had anal intercourse performed on me approximately _____ times.

15. I have been pressured into having sex against my will approximately _____ times.

16. I have been involved in an ongoing sexual relationship (hooked up) with another inmate? ____ Yes ____ No If yes, for how long? _____

17. Are you currently hooked up? ____ Yes ____ No

18. Outside of prison I have engaged in sexual activity with other males on approximately _____ occasions.

19. Approximately how old were you at the time of your first sexual experience with another male? _____

20. I consider myself to be: ____ Heterosexual ____ Bisexual ____ Homosexual

## Survey of Homosexuals in Prison

This is an anonymous survey. Please answer each question by filling in the blank or circling the appropriate response. *Do not* write your name on this paper.

1. What is your age? _____
2. What is your race? ____ Black ____ Caucasian ____ Hispanic ____ Other
3. What crime were you sent to prison for? _____
4. How long a sentence did you receive? _____
5. What is the date on your I.D. card? _____
6. Is this your: ____ First ____ Second ____ Third prison term?
7. What was your age at the time of your first sexual experience with another male? _____
8. At approximately what age did you "come out" or decide that you were a homosexual? _____

*Since coming to prison this term:*

9. I have had sexual experiences with approximately _____ different inmates.
10. I have been orally copulated approximately_____ times.
11. I have performed anal intercourse on another inmate approximately _____ times.
12. I have orally copulated another inmate approximately _____ times.
13. I have had anal intercourse performed on me approximately _____ times.

14. I have been pressured into having sex with another inmate, against my will, approximately _____ times.

15. I have been physically assaulted by another inmate _____ times.

16. I have received _____ 115s for sexual conduct or compromising position.

*Respond to the following statements by circling the number that most accurately reflects your feelings or experience.*

> 1—strongly agree; 2—agree somewhat; 3—don't know; 4—disagree somewhat; 5—strongly disagree

17. I am a homosexual.     1   2   3   4   5

18. I am a bisexual.     1   2   3   4   5

19. I act more feminine than masculine.     1   2   3   4   5

20. I would rather be straight.     1   2   3   4   5

21. I would rather be a female.     1   2   3   4   5

22. I would like to be more masculine.     1   2   3   4   5

23. I am happy and satisfied with my sexual identity.     1   2   3   4   5

24. Homosexual inmates are looked down on and treated with disrespect by other inmates.     1   2   3   4   5

25. The staff is sensitive to the problems of homosexual inmates and makes an effort to protect them.     1   2   3   4   5

26. I am frequently pressured sexually by other inmates.     1   2   3   4   5

27. The staff tends to tolerate homosexual relationships between
inmates.                                          1   2   3   4   5

28. I am hooked up with one other
inmate who protects me.                           1   2   3   4   5

29. Homosexual inmates are looked
down on and treated with dis-
respect by the staff.                             1   2   3   4   5

30. I am involved or have been
involved in some form of
therapy.                                          1   2   3   4   5

31. I prefer "straight trade" for sex-
ual partners.                                     1   2   3   4   5

32. I prefer masculine homosexuals
for sexual partners.                              1   2   3   4   5

33. I prefer feminine homosexuals
for sexual partners.                              1   2   3   4   5

34. I often have sex with someone
for profit (commissary, etc.).                    1   2   3   4   5

35. I prefer giving head to being
fucked.                                           1   2   3   4   5

36. I always take the passive role
when having sex.                                  1   2   3   4   5

37. On the streets I frequently dress
in drag.                                          1   2   3   4   5

38. Most of my sexual partners con-
sider themselves to be straight.                  1   2   3   4   5

39. I have more sex in prison than
on the street.                                    1   2   3   4   5

40. I have better sex in prison than
on the street.                                    1   2   3   4   5

41. Most of my sexual partners
    respect me as a person.                    1   2   3   4   5
42. I have often been pressured into
    having sex with someone who I
    would rather not have been
    involved with.                             1   2   3   4   5

# Appendix B

## Tables

Table 1. Age in Years

| Age | Sample data | | Total prison (1979) | | Total prison (1980) | |
|---|---|---|---|---|---|---|
| | No. | % | No. | % | No. | % |
| Under 20 | 0 | 0 | 25 | 1.0 | 30 | 1.1 |
| 20–24 | 48 | 24.0 | 635 | 24.9 | 621 | 23.8 |
| 25–29 | 56 | 28.0 | 757 | 29.7 | 753 | 28.9 |
| 30–34 | 40 | 20.0 | 480 | 18.8 | 542 | 20.8 |
| 35–39 | 21 | 10.5 | 278 | 10.9 | 264 | 10.1 |
| 40–44 | 17 | 8.5 | 166 | 6.5 | 188 | 7.2 |
| 45–49 | 11 | 5.5 | 88 | 3.5 | 78 | 3.0 |
| 50–54 | 4 | 2.0 | 48 | 1.9 | 67 | 2.6 |
| 55–59 | 3 | 1.5 | 37 | 1.5 | 23 | 0.9 |
| 60 and over | 0 | 0 | 33 | 1.3 | 41 | 1.6 |
| *Median age* | 29 | | 29 | | 29 | |
| Total | 200 | 100.0 | 2547 | 100.0 | 2607 | 100.0 |

Table 2. Ethnic Group Identification

| Race | Sample data | | Total prison (1979) | | Total prison (1980) | |
|---|---|---|---|---|---|---|
| | No. | % | No. | % | No. | % |
| Caucasian | 88 | 44.0 | 1282 | 50.3 | 1148 | 44.0 |
| Mexican-American | 39 | 19.5 | 356 | 14.0 | 504 | 19.4 |
| Black | 70 | 35.0 | 868 | 34.1 | 916 | 35.1 |
| Other | 3 | 1.5 | 41 | 1.6 | 39 | 1.5 |
| Total | 200 | 100.0 | 2547 | 100.0 | 2607 | 100.0 |

Table 3. Offense

| Offense | Sample data | | Total prison (1979) | | Total prison (1980) | |
|---|---|---|---|---|---|---|
| | No. | % | No. | % | No. | % |
| Homicide | 30 | 15.0 | 548 | 21.5 | 555 | 21.3 |
| Robbery | 53 | 26.5 | 573 | 22.5 | 605 | 23.2 |
| Assault | 16 | 8.0 | 221 | 8.7 | 217 | 8.3 |
| Burglary | 37 | 18.5 | 319 | 12.5 | 304 | 11.7 |
| Theft (except auto) | 11 | 5.5 | 67 | 2.6 | 79 | 3.0 |
| Auto theft | 7 | 3.5 | 45 | 1.8 | 43 | 1.6 |
| Forgery and checks | 9 | 4.5 | 22 | 0.9 | 33 | 1.3 |
| Rape | 8 | 4.0 | 281 | 11.0 | 310 | 11.9 |
| Other sex | 7 | 3.5 | 187 | 7.3 | 195 | 7.5 |
| Drugs | 20 | 10.0 | 149 | 5.9 | 122 | 4.7 |
| Other | 2 | 1.0 | 135 | 5.3 | 144 | 5.5 |
| Total | 200 | 100.0 | 2547 | 100.0 | 2607 | 100.0 |

*Table 4.*  Term in Prison

| Term | Sample data | | Prison data (1980) | |
|------|------|------|------|------|
|  | No. | % | No. | % |
| First | 132 | 66.0 | 1743 | 66.9 |
| Second | 46 | 23.0 | 557 | 21.4 |
| Third | 17 | 8.5 | 191 | 7.3 |
| Fourth or more | 5 | 2.5 | 116 | 4.4 |
| Total | 200 | 100.0 | 2607 | 100.0 |

*Table 5.*  Length of Time Served

| Time served | Sample data | |
|------|------|------|
|  | No. | % |
| 1 and 2 years | 38 | 19.0 |
| 3 and 4 years | 84 | 42.0 |
| 5 and 6 years | 28 | 14.0 |
| 7 and 8 years | 26 | 13.0 |
| 9 and 10 years | 16 | 8.0 |
| Over 10 years | 8 | 4.0 |
| Total | 200 | 100.0 |

*Table 6.*  Marital Status

| Marital status | Sample data | |
|------|------|------|
|  | No. | % |
| Single | 105 | 52.5 |
| Married | 55 | 27.5 |
| Separated | 16 | 8.0 |
| Divorced | 24 | 12.0 |
| Total | 200 | 100.0 |

### Table 7. Number of Sexual Partners by Sexual Orientation

| Reported number of sexual partners | Orientation | | | Row totals[a] |
|---|---|---|---|---|
| | Heterosexual | Bisexual | Homosexual | |
| None | 70 | 0 | 0 | 70 |
| | 44.6% | 0% | 0% | 35.0% |
| 1–3 | 68 | 4 | 0 | 72 |
| | 43.3% | 18.2% | 0% | 36.0% |
| 4–6 | 15 | 10 | 2 | 27 |
| | 9.6% | 45.5% | 9.5% | 13.5% |
| 7–9 | 1 | 2 | 2 | 5 |
| | 0.6% | 9.1% | 9.5% | 2.5% |
| 10–20 | 2 | 6 | 11 | 19 |
| | 1.3% | 27.3% | 52.4% | 9.5% |
| Over 20 | 1 | 0 | 6 | 7 |
| | 0.6% | 0% | 28.6% | 3.5% |
| Column totals[a] | 157 | 22 | 21 | 200 |
| | 78.5% | 11.0% | 10.5% | 100.0% |

[a]Raw chi square = 161.15343 with 10 D.F.; siginificance = 0.

### Table 8. Frequency of Being Orally Copulated

| Reported being orally copulated | Orientation | | | Row totals[a] |
|---|---|---|---|---|
| | Heterosexual | Bisexual | Homosexual | |
| None | 88 | 0 | 9 | 97 |
| | 56.1% | 0% | 42.9% | 48.5% |
| 1–3 times | 37 | 0 | 4 | 41 |
| | 23.6% | 0% | 19.0% | 20.5% |
| 4–6 times | 9 | 1 | 2 | 12 |
| | 5.7% | 4.5% | 9.5% | 6.0% |
| 7–9 times | 3 | 0 | 0 | 3 |
| | 1.9% | 0% | 0% | 1.5% |
| 10–20 times | 15 | 8 | 6 | 29 |
| | 9.6% | 36.4% | 28.6% | 14.5% |
| Over 20 times | 5 | 13 | 0 | 18 |
| | 3.2% | 59.1% | 0% | 9.0% |
| Column totals[a] | 157 | 22 | 21 | 200 |
| | 78.5% | 11.2% | 10.5% | 100.0% |

[a]Raw chi square = 101.14986 with 10 D.F.; siginificance = 0.

Table 9. Frequency of Performing Anal Penetration

| Reported performing anal penetration | Orientation | | | Row totals[a] |
|---|---|---|---|---|
| | Heterosexual | Bisexual | Homosexual | |
| None | 111 | 0 | 12 | 123 |
| | 70.7% | 0% | 57.1% | 61.5% |
| 1–3 times | 26 | 0 | 4 | 30 |
| | 16.6% | 0% | 19.0% | 15.0% |
| 4–6 times | 7 | 0 | 3 | 10 |
| | 4.5% | 0% | 14.3% | 5.0% |
| 7-9times | 0 | 1 | 0 | 1 |
| | 0% | 4.5% | 0% | 0.5% |
| 10–20 times | 11 | 12 | 2 | 25 |
| | 7.0% | 54.5% | 9.5% | 12.5% |
| Over 20 times | 2 | 9 | 0 | 11 |
| | 1.3% | 40.9% | 0% | 5.5% |
| Column totals[a] | 157 | 22 | 21 | 200 |
| | 78.5% | 11.0% | 10.5% | 100.0% |

[a]Raw chi square = 123.90291 with 10 D.F.; siginificance = 0.

Table 10. Frequency of Performing Oral Copulation

| Reported performing oral copulation | Orientation | | | Row totals[a] |
|---|---|---|---|---|
| | Heterosexual | Bisexual | Homosexual | |
| None | 148 | 9 | 2 | 159 |
| | 94.3% | 40.9% | 9.5% | 79.5% |
| 1–3 times | 8 | 3 | 1 | 12 |
| | 5.1% | 13.6% | 4.8% | 6.0% |
| 4–6 times | 1 | 2 | 0 | 3 |
| | 0.6% | 9.1% | 0% | 1.5% |
| 7–9 times | 0 | 0 | 0 | 0 |
| | 0% | 0% | 0% | 0% |
| 10–20 times | 0 | 5 | 2 | 7 |
| | 0% | 22.7% | 9.5% | 3.5% |
| 21–50 times | 0 | 3 | 6 | 9 |
| | 0% | 13.6% | 28.6% | 4.5% |
| Over 50 times | 0 | 0 | 10 | 10 |
| | 0% | 0% | 47.6% | 5.0% |
| Column totals[a] | 157 | 22 | 21 | 200 |
| | 78.5% | 11.0% | 10.5% | 100.0% |

[a]Raw chi square = 187.64822 with 10 D.F.; significance = 0.

Table 11.  Frequency of Being Anally Penetrated

| Reported having been anally penetrated | Orientation | | | Row totals[a] |
|---|---|---|---|---|
| | Heterosexual | Bisexual | Homosexual | |
| None | 144 | 14 | 1 | 159 |
| | 91.7% | 63.6% | 4.8% | 79.5% |
| 1–3 times | 9 | 4 | 0 | 13 |
| | 5.7% | 18.2% | 0% | 6.5% |
| 4–6 times | 4 | 1 | 0 | 5 |
| | 2.5% | 4.5% | 0% | 2.5% |
| 7–9 times | 0 | 0 | 0 | 0 |
| | 0% | 0% | 0% | 0% |
| 10–20 times | 0 | 2 | 3 | 5 |
| | 0% | 9.1% | 14.3% | 2.5% |
| 21–50 times | 0 | 1 | 5 | 6 |
| | 0% | 4.5% | 23.8% | 3.0% |
| Over 50 times | 0 | 0 | 12 | 12 |
| | 0% | 0% | 57.1% | 6.0% |
| Column totals[a] | 157 | 22 | 21 | 200 |
| | 78.5% | 11.0% | 10.5% | 100.0% |

[a]Raw chi square = 182.31988 with 10 D.F.; significance = 0

Table 12.   Summary Table

| Reported having performed this sexual act | Orientation | | | Row totals |
|---|---|---|---|---|
| | Heterosexual | Bisexual | Homosexual | |
| Prison sex | 87 (157) | 22 | 21 | 130 |
| | 55.4% | 100.0% | 100.0% | 65.0% |
| Being orally copulated | 69 | 22 | 12 | 103 |
| | 43.9% | 100.0% | 57.1% | 51.5% |
| Performing anal penetration | 46 | 22 | 9 | 77 |
| | 29.3% | 100.0% | 42.9% | 38.5% |
| Performing oral copulation | 9 | 13 | 19 | 41 |
| | 5.7% | 59.1% | 90.5% | 20.5% |
| Having been anally penetrated | 13 | 8 | 20 | 41 |
| | 8.3% | 36.4% | 95.2% | 20.5% |

Table 13.   Sexual Behavior by Marital Status for Self-Defined Heterosexuals

| Marital status | Reported having sex | Reported not having sex | Row totals[a] |
|---|---|---|---|
| Single | 37 | 27 | 64 |
| | 24.8% | 18.1% | 42.9% |
| Married | 32 | 22 | 54 |
| | 21.5% | 14.8% | 36.3% |
| Separated | 5 | 6 | 11 |
| | 3.4% | 4.0% | 7.4% |
| Divorced | 9 | 11 | 20 |
| | 6.0% | 7.4% | 13.4% |
| Column totals[a] | 83 | 66 | 149 |
| | 55.7% | 44.3% | 100.0% |

[a]Raw chi square = 1.791 with 3 D.F.; not significant = 0.05.

*Table 14.* Sexual Behavior and Conjugal Visits for Married Self-Defined Heterosexuals

| Conjugal visits | Reported having sex | Reported not having sex | Row totals[a] |
|---|---|---|---|
| Received visits | 23<br>46.0% | 8<br>16.0% | 31<br>62.0% |
| Did not receive visits | 8<br>16.0% | 11<br>22.0% | 19<br>38.0% |
| Column totals[a] | 31<br>62.0% | 19<br>38.0% | 50<br>100% |

[a]Raw chi square = 4.063 with 1 D.F.; significance = 0.05.

*Table 15.* Ethnicity and Patterns of Sexual Behavior of Heterosexuals

| Reported having performed this sexual act | Ethnicity | | | Row totals |
|---|---|---|---|---|
| | Black (N = 52) | Caucasian (N = 71) | Mexican (N = 31) | |
| Prison sex[a] | 42<br>80.8% | 27<br>38.0% | 17<br>54.8% | 86<br>55.8% |
| Being orally copulated | 32<br>61.5% | 21<br>29.6% | 16<br>51.6% | 69<br>44.8% |
| Performing anal penetration | 24<br>46.2% | 12<br>16.9% | 10<br>32.3% | 46<br>29.9% |
| Performing oral copulation | 2<br>3.8% | 7<br>9.9% | 0<br>0% | 9<br>5.7% |
| Having been anally penetrated | 3<br>5.8% | 8<br>11.3% | 1<br>3.4% | 12<br>7.8% |

[a]Raw chi square = 35.52848 with 10 D.F.; significance = 0.0001.

*Table 16.* Ethnicity and Patterns of Sexual Behavior for Bisexuals

| Reported having performed this sexual act | Ethnicity | | | Row totals |
|---|---|---|---|---|
| | Black (N = 9) | Caucasian (N = 10) | Mexican (N = 3) | |
| Prison Sex | 9 100.0% | 10 100.0% | 3 100.0% | 22 100.0% |
| Being orally copulated | 9 100.0% | 10 100.0% | 3 100.0% | 22 100.0% |
| Performing anal penetration | 9 100.0% | 10 100.0% | 3 100.0% | 22 100.0% |
| Performing oral copulation | 2 22.2% | 9 90.0% | 2 66.6% | 13 59.9% |
| Having been anally penetrated | 0 0% | 7 70.0% | 1 33.3% | 8 36.8% |

*Table 17.* Ethnicity and Patterns of Sexual Behavior for Homosexuals

| Reported having performed this sexual act | Ethnicity | | | Row totals |
|---|---|---|---|---|
| | Black (N = 37) | Caucasian (N = 26) | Mexican (N = 17) | |
| Being orally copulated | 19 51.4% | 16 61.5% | 4 23.5% | 39 48.7% |
| Performing anal penetration | 19 51.4% | 11 42.3% | 3 17.6% | 33 41.3% |
| Performing oral copulation | 34 91.9% | 26 100.0% | 16 94.1% | 76 95.0% |
| Having been anally penetrated | 37 100.0% | 25 96.2% | 17 100.0% | 79 98.8% |

*Table 18.*   Feminine-Defined Homosexuals and Reported Passivity in
Anal Sex

| Reported instances of having been anally penetrated | More feminine than masculine | Not sure | More masculine than feminine | Row totals[a] |
|---|---|---|---|---|
| None | 0 | 1 | 0 | 1 |
| | 0% | 9.1% | 0% | 1.2% |
| 1–25 times | 7 | 0 | 12 | 19 |
| | 15.6% | 0% | 50.0% | 23.8% |
| 26–50 times | 12 | 6 | 8 | 26 |
| | 26.7% | 54.5% | 33.3% | 32.5% |
| 51–100 times | 8 | 3 | 1 | 12 |
| | 17.8% | 27.3% | 4.2% | 15.0% |
| 101–150 times | 10 | 1 | 3 | 14 |
| | 22.2% | 9.1% | 12.5% | 17.5% |
| Over 150 times | 8 | 0 | 0 | 8 |
| | 17.8% | 0% | 0% | 10.0% |
| Column totals[a] | 45 | 11 | 24 | 80 |
| | 56.3% | 13.7% | 30.0% | 100.0% |

[a]Raw chi square = 30.03867 with 10 D.F.; significance = 0.0008.

Table 19.   Homosexual Experience or Feelings in Prison

| Statements concerning homosexual feelings | Agree | Not sure | Disagree |
|---|---|---|---|
| *Sexual Identity* | | | |
| I am a homosexual. | 80 100.0% | 0 0% | 0 0% |
| I am a bisexual. | 15 18.8% | 2 2.5% | 63 78.7% |
| I act more feminine than masculine. | 45 56.3% | 11 13.7% | 24 30.0% |
| I am happy and satisfied with my sexual identity. | 61 76.3% | 9 11.3% | 10 12.4% |
| I would rather be straight. | 1 1.3% | 12 15.0% | 67 83.7% |
| I would rather be a female. | 10 12.5% | 8 10.0% | 62 77.5% |
| I would rather be more masculine. | 11 13.7% | 23 28.8% | 46 57.5% |
| *Treatment in Prison* | | | |
| The staff is sensitive to the problems of homosexual inmates and makes an attempt to protect them. | 28 35.0% | 14 17.5% | 38 47.5% |
| Homosexual inmates are looked down upon and treated with disrespect by the staff. | 34 42.5% | 18 22.5% | 28 35.0% |
| The staff tends to tolerate homosexual relationships between inmates. | 47 58.7% | 15 18.8% | 18 22.5% |
| Homosexual inmates are looked down upon and treated with disrespect by other inmates. | 62 77.5% | 13 16.2% | 5 6.3% |
| I am hooked up with one other inmate who protects me. | 70 87.5% | 1 1.2% | 9 11.2% |
| I am frequently pressured sexually by other inmates. | 42 52.5% | 4 5.0% | 34 42.5% |
| I have often been pressured into having sex. | 33 41.3% | 8 10.0% | 39 48.7% |

*(Continued)*

*Table 19.*   (*Continued*)

| Statements concerning homosexual feelings | Agree | Not sure | Disagree |
| --- | --- | --- | --- |
| I am involved or have been involved in some form of therapy. | 19<br>23.8% | 0<br>0% | 61<br>76.3% |
| *Sexual Experiences in Prison* | | | |
| I prefer "straight trade" for sexual partners. | 35<br>43.8% | 12<br>15.0% | 33<br>41.3% |
| I prefer masculine homosexuals for sexual partners. | 71<br>88.8% | 5<br>6.3% | 4<br>5.0% |
| I prefer feminine homosexuals for sexual partners. | 10<br>12.5% | 2<br>2.5% | 68<br>85.0% |
| I often have sex with someone for profit. | 28<br>35.0% | 3<br>3.7% | 49<br>61.2% |
| I prefer performing oral copulation to being anally penetrated. | 21<br>26.2% | 27<br>33.7% | 32<br>40.0% |
| I always take the passive role when having sex. | 58<br>72.5% | 7<br>8.8% | 15<br>18.8% |
| On the streets I frequently dress in drag. | 27<br>33.7% | 3<br>3.7% | 50<br>62.5% |
| I have more sex in prison than on the street. | 19<br>23.8% | 14<br>17.5% | 47<br>58.7% |
| I have better sex in prison than on the street. | 11<br>13.7% | 7<br>8.8% | 62<br>77.4% |
| Most of my sexual partners consider themselves to be straight. | 71<br>88.8% | 0<br>0% | 9<br>11.2% |
| Most of my sexual partners respect me as a person. | 30<br>37.5% | 29<br>36.2% | 21<br>26.2% |

*Table 20.* Feminine-Defined Homosexuals by Race or Ethnicity

| Act more feminine than masculine | Ethnicity | | | Row totals[a] |
|---|---|---|---|---|
| | Black | Caucasian | Mexican | |
| Agree | 24 | 7 | 14 | 45 |
| | 64.9% | 26.9% | 82.4% | 56.3% |
| Not sure | 6 | 4 | 1 | 11 |
| | 16.2% | 15.4% | 5.9% | 13.7% |
| Disagree | 7 | 15 | 2 | 24 |
| | 18.9 | 57.7% | 11.8% | 30.0% |
| Column totals[a] | 37 | 26 | 17 | 80 |
| | 46.2% | 32.5% | 21.2% | 100.0% |

[a]Raw chi square = 17.54722 with 4 D.F.; significance = 0.0015.

*Table 21.* Homosexuals Coerced into Sex by Race or Ethnicity

| Have been pressured into sex | Ethnicity | | | Row totals[a] |
|---|---|---|---|---|
| | Black | Caucasian | Mexican | |
| Agree | 10 | 17 | 6 | 33 |
| | 27.0% | 65.4% | 35.3% | 41.3% |
| Not sure | 2 | 3 | 3 | 8 |
| | 5.4% | 11.5% | 17.6% | 10.0% |
| Disagree | 25 | 6 | 8 | 39 |
| | 67.6% | 23.1% | 47.1% | 48.7% |
| Column totals[a] | 37 | 26 | 17 | 80 |
| | 46.2% | 32.5% | 21.2% | 100.0% |

[a]Raw chi square = 13.68157 with 4 D.F.; significance = 0.0084.

# Index

Homosexuals (*cont.*)
  sexual experiences in prison,
    125–129, 135–141
  sexual identity of, 130–132
  sexual pressure and, 127–128,
    134, 135, 140
  situational, 15, 37
  staff attitudes toward, 42, 187–
    204, 231
  stigma attached to, 44–45
  survey of background and
    activity, 122–125
  treatment in prison, 132–135
  types of, 143–164
  use of term, 3
  *See also* Gay, specific topics
Hook-up
  definition of term, 2
  *See also* Relationships, sexual
Hustling, 24, 58, 59, 76, 136

Importation model of prison
  behavior, 43–44, 57, 62
Inmate attitudes toward
  homosexuality, 167–186
  older prisoners, 168–177
  religious leaders, 177–186
"Inmates," distinctions between
  "convicts" and, 172–174
Interracial assault. *See* Black
  prisoners,rape and; White
  prisoners,sexual
  victimization and
Interracial pairings, 60
Interviews, 6–8

Jobs, 28–29, 32, 34–35
  older prisoners and, 174–175
Jockers (studs)
  definition of term, 3
  prison sexual code as
    determined by, 44

Jockers (*cont.*)
  as protection, 18, 19
  ramifications of sexual
    victimization for, 115
  sexual orientation of, 15–16
  *See also* specific topics

Keestering, 30
Keester stash, 30
Kids
  definition of term, 3
  *See also* Punks
Kissing (mugging), 22

Labels, ambiguity of, 16
Library, 32, 36
Loneliness, 77–78
Lower-class (lower-income)
  background, 21, 44, 45, 58, 60

Machismo, 15, 17, 20, 44
Marital status, 48–49, 55–56, 231
  of punks, 100
Masculinity (manhood), 15–17,
  44, 45, 115
  "cult" of, 21
  sexual assault and loss of, 99, 117
Masturbation, frequency of, 50
Media, 221–222, 225–226
Metropolitan Community Church
  (MCC), 217–219, 221, 223
Mexican-American (Chicano)
  prisoners, 197, 199, 231
  barrio culture, 57–59
  bisexuals, 64–67
  effeminate homosexuals, 20–21, 45
  homosexual behavior and, 45
  homosexuals, 122, 123, 126, 128,
    130–139
  older, 169–171, 175
  sexual behavior survey and,
    57–63